One Man's River

THE CLYDE IN PICTURES

1920 - 1980

City of New York outward bound in 1949.

One Man's River

THE CLYDE IN PICTURES
1920 - 1980

The Dan McDonald Collection

BY LEN PATERSON

Published by House of Lochar
in collaboration with
Glasgow Museums

Glasgow Museums
will receive all
Royalties from the sale of this book

By the same author
Twelve Hundred Miles for Thirty Shillings
Only Thirty Birthdays
The Light in the Glens

By Dan McDonald
The Clyde Puffer

ISBN 1 899863 49 4

Designed and typeset by Buffey & Buffey,
Coggeshall, Essex
Repro by Facsimile Graphics,
Coggeshall, Essex
Printed in Great Britain
by Redwood Books, Trowbridge
for House of Lochar
Colonsay, Argyll

Contents

Acknowledgement 7

Captions to Pictures 9

Map of the Clyde 10 & 11

Daniel McDonald 13

The Last Days of Sail 21

Lines of Yards 37

Doon the Watter 63

Across the Watter 79

The Watter, Deep and Clean 87

Pulling and Pushing 95

Small was Equally Beautiful 109

The Clyde Puffer 119

The Rivers Royalty 131

Epilogue 144

For Sean and Caitriona

Acknowledgements

My thanks are due to many people who helped in the production of this book.

It would have been well nigh impossible to compile this book but for the dedicated efforts of the good folk at The Ballast Trust, Bill Lind, Duncan McKenzie and Mrs Colquhoun. Bill Lind not only rescued the McDonald negatives from obscurity but he and his staff gave me encouragement and practical support throughout the exercise.

At Glasgow Museums, Alistair Smith and Deborah Haase helped me with access to the McDonald notebooks and Darryl Mead smoothed the path of the project within the organisation. The production of prints from the negatives, sometimes no easy task, was expertly and enthusiastically carried out by Alan Broadfoot (to whom a special thanks) at the Photographic Department at the Burrell Collection.

Sue and Richard Buffey were great supporters from the outset once they had seen the quality of the McDonald pictures and they have contributed their unique talents to the visual impact of the book.

Far from least, (*pace* her position in this list) is Georgina Hobhouse, of the House of Lochar, for whose editorial work on the text and captions I am truly grateful. As ever, it was fun, Georgina.

The North British Railway Company's *Talisman* was built on the Clyde by A. & J. Inglis in 1896. Fast for her time, her top speed was over 18 knots, she was a minelayer in World War 1.

She had an overall length of 215 feet, a beam of 23 feet, and a draft of 7.5 feet. Had she been box-shaped the volume enclosed by these dimensions would have been 37,000 cubic feet. At 100 cubic feet per ton (see opposite) she would have had a grt of 370. But her fine lines at the bow and stern meant that her volume was lower and this accounts for the actual grt being less at 293. Increasing the beam and draft of a ship could put up her grt quite dramatically.

This may help the reader to use grt, to make comparisons between ship sizes.

Talisman 1896/290

Captions to Pictures

The strength of the book is the photographs and very few are not of ships. Some people who are attracted to pictures of boats insist on being given, above all else, all the technical details; precise dimensions, tonnages, launch dates, owners, builders, engine makers, horsepower etc. In a book of well over one hundred pictures such repetitive detail would be indigestible and get in the way of describing a larger picture, that of the story of the vessel and her historical context.

At the end of each caption is the name of the ship and two figures. In the example opposite, of *Talisman,* the "1896/290" means that the vessel was built in 1896 and that her gross rated tonnage was approximately 290. We believe that this gives the reader a convenient shorthand message about the ship. The true shipping buff will in any case know where to find all the details that he wants.

There can be debate amongst the purists as to whether launch or completion (i.e. acceptance by the owner) date should be quoted. As far as we know we have used launch date.

Gross rated tonnage, grt, is now called gross tonnage, gt, in shipping circles. It is a measurement of a ship's volume. Each 100 cubic feet is called a gross ton. The figure will give the reader an idea of a ship's size relative to others.

Frankly, grt is not particularly meaningful for non-cargo carriers like tugs and ferries and not at all for warships. The tonnages quoted for Royal Navy ships are the displacements, (read up on the Archimedes Principle) and these were not fixed but could vary depending on a variety of factors.

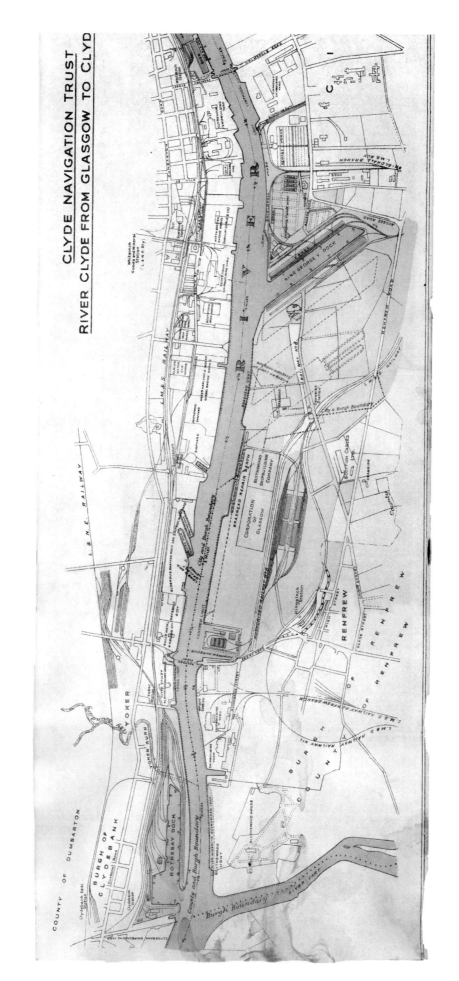

The River in 1945
Rothesay Dock to Shieldhall Wharf

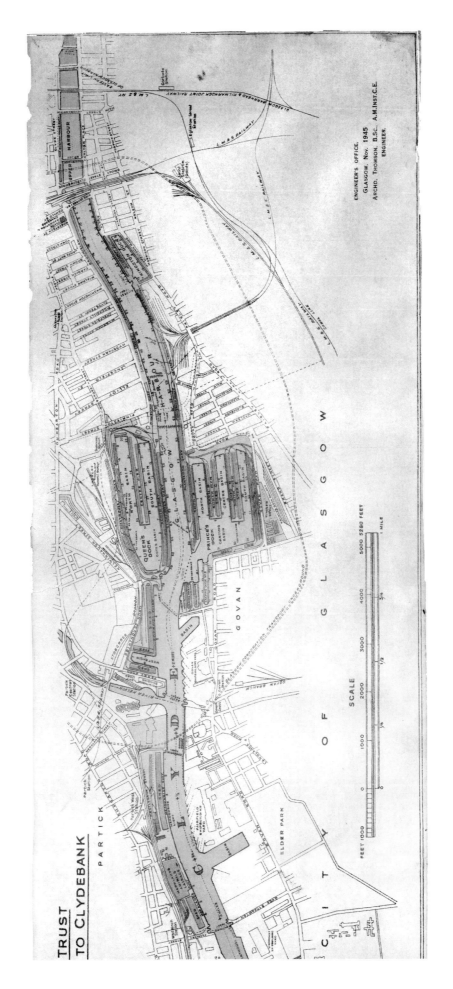

The River in 1945
Shieldhall Wharf to the Upper Harbour

Daniel McDonald
(1899-1988)

I first met Dan McDonald in the offices of Glenlight Shipping Ltd. in the mid-1970s when he was working on the production of his famous book "The Clyde Puffer". This book's multitude of readers will know that he was an accomplished photographer. Most of the better pictures in his book were taken by McDonald himself.

He was well known to Glenlight's staff as a man who had often taken his holidays on the company's puffers. Theoretically he sailed as a supernumary, but in the eyes of the crews he was really one of their own. Many people with romantic notions of West Highland shipping wanted to be taken on a puffer for a vacation, but a small working ship with cramped accommodation and idiosyncratic personnel is no place for a landlubber with fanciful ideas about a summer cruise. Few were granted the privilege. A sense of who would fit in and who would not was well developed by the Glenlight staff. Even when an applicant met the unwritten criteria the chemistry between visitor and crew was not always right and some were discouraged, by various means, from taking a second voyage. There were no such problems with McDonald who instinctively built a rapport with crews. Dan McDonald was always welcomed on board - and so was his camera.

He made as many as seventeen trips on various puffers between 1949 and 1972 and he captured the essence of the men and the ships. The photographs in this volume testify to that. But his obvious love for these small ships was just part of his greater love for all things of the sea. He not only photographed puffers for over twenty years, he also photographed the River Clyde, its Estuary and everything that floated on it for sixty years until about 1980. He did it as an aid to cataloguing the ships that he observed and studied as his life-long hobby. In so doing he captured the Clyde on film from an unique perspective over a period that covered its inter-war bustle, when it still had the appearance and trappings of its heyday, to the desolation of the 1980s when it had lost most of its economic and intellectual drive.

Dan McDonald on board the puffer, *Glenshira*, in August 1965.

Thus he observed through his lens the last days of sail, the birth of the Queens (all three), paddlers "doon the watter", the fall of steam, the rise of diesel, the first hovercraft, famous shipping lines and renowned building yards. The result was a collection of over 5,000 black and white negatives. Those reproduced here are therefore only a small, but hopefully representative, sample of that considerable output.

Dan McDonald was born in Glasgow on the 13th of November 1899 and was brought up on the South bank of the Clyde in the Kingston area of the city - no more than half a mile from the stretch of water that fascinated him all his life. He was educated at Shields Road Primary School from where he won a bursary to Bellahouston Academy, which was then a fee-paying school. Clearly he was an intelligent youngster. His preferred readings were the works of Captain Marryat, Jack London and Joseph Conrad. Little wonder then that he was "boat daft", in the vernacular that the Glaswegian uses to describe an obsession with ships.

He also won a scholarship to Glasgow University but did not take it up. Perhaps World War I intervened but perhaps he had already decided that the academic life was not for him. He had joined the staff of Glasgow Corporation Parks Department, where he was to spend all his working life, shortly before he was conscripted into the army at the age of eighteen. He served with the King's Own Scottish Borderers and with the Glasgow Division of the Highland Light Infantry before being demobilised in 1919.

It was soon after this, for the earliest negatives in the collection date from 1920, that he began to take photographs as a way of enhancing the records of the ships that he was studying. Family tradition has it that he was given his first camera as a birthday present when he was eight. (If this was so it was an imaginative gift in a turn of the century working class family.) He was still taking photographs in August 1980, when he was nearly 81 years old, and the last picture in the Collection, that of *mv Tipperary*, was assigned the number 2868. Since he often took more than one shot of a subject and gave all those of the same ship the same negative number the total in the collection in fact exceeds the 5,000 mark. For example there are twelve studies of the square rigged sailing ship *Grace Harwar*.

Dan McDonald's yacht, the four ton sloop *Ailie*, in the Kyles of Bute. He shared the ownership of her with a friend, Andrew Roulston.

Campbeltown fishing vessels at Bridge Wharf in 1939. At this time the Fish Market across the river at Clyde Street was still functioning and the Estuary boats came all the way into the City to deliver their catches.

When not spending his leisure hours tramping up and down the Clydeside quays, camera in hand, McDonald was giving talks, often illustrated with his own photographs, to local marine and historical societies, writing articles on shipping matters and corresponding, literally on a world-wide basis, with other ship enthusiasts. Such was his standing as a maritime lecturer and researcher that he was made an honorary member of the Cape Horners' and Master Mariners' Club. This was an unique honour for one who was not a professional seaman.

His frustration at not "going to the sea" was alleviated somewhat by the pleasure that he got from sailing on the Clyde and the West Coast of Scotland in his yacht *Ailie*, which he owned jointly with a friend. (When pouring over his notebooks I came across a receipt, tucked between two pages, for the cost of *Ailie's* passage through the Crinan Canal in 1927. The charge for the four ton sloop was twenty-seven shillings, say £1.35 in today's decimal coin.) He married in 1930 and had one daughter, Muriel, who was to become his companion and nurse during his ill health at the end of his life.

His photographic activities were curtailed for security reasons by World War II (there are no pictures from October 1939 until July of 1945), but he was active enough in the Local Defence Volunteers and the Home Guard throughout the hostilities. As soon as he could he was out taking pictures again in spite of the post-war shortage of photographic materials and the decade up to the late 1950s was probably his most productive.

The reason for his visit to the Glenlight offices in 1970-something was to talk about photographs for his book "The Clyde Puffer" and we were able to lend him one or two

This silhouette was on the cover of Dan McDonald's 1977 book "The Clyde Puffer". We can do no better than quote:

"The *Turk* built by John Hay & Sons in 1929 sets out from Yorkhill for her day's work on the river taking bunker coal to the dredgers and their attendant hopper barges."

Turk 1929/70

views of Greenock in the 1890s which subsequently appeared in the finished book in 1977. (Now published by House of Lochar, ISBN 1 899863 12 5). The compliment was returned posthumously nearly twenty years later when my history of the puffer trade, "The Light in the Glens" came out (also House of Lochar, ISBN 0 899863 14 1). About a quarter of its photographic material came from the Dan McDonald Collection.

While searching for pictures for the book I had come across the Collection in Glasgow's Museum of Transport and as I trawled through it looking for puffer pictures I was struck not only by the quality of his work but by the content and nature of it. Here amongst many photographs on many maritime subjects was the history of the Clyde from 1920 to 1980 in all its variety. I thought it deserved as wide an audience as possible - and the idea of this book was conceived.

The sailing ship *Medea* was built by Barclay Curle in 1868 at their original yard at Stobcross. (They had to vacate the yard when Queen's Dock was constructed.) The principal interest of the picture is that the demand for berths in the River was so high in 1928 that ships had to be moored in mid-river.

Dan McDonald's health had deteriorated shortly after the publication of his puffer book and in 1980 he ceased taking photographs. He had expressed a little sadness about the final form of his book. He and his publisher had taken rather different views of its contents and the commercial view prevailed. It is a slim volume rich in pictures and modest in its technical descriptions. He could have written, and certainly wished to have written, a more detailed and interesting commentary on the development of the coasters than actually was printed.

He died on April 4th 1988. After his death his collection of photographs, newspaper cuttings, notebooks and maritime ephemera, some fifteen thousand items, came into the possession of the Museum of Transport in Glasgow.

The photographs, the treasure of the Collection, were fixed into thirty-nine board-bound, 12cm x 20cm notebooks each containing around one hundred pages of photographs. The pages were slit to take the corners of what appear to be contact prints of each picture and there were two or at most three pictures to each page. Most are approximately 5cm square which suggests that they were taken on the old 120 film format although some are 5cm x 7.5cm. We can only guess at what make of camera he used but the sharpness of the focus and the quality of the tones indicate that he used equipment more sophisticated than the box camera. Some of the negatives from the 1920s are glass so at that time he was probably using some form of plate camera.

The photographic process itself must have stimulated his interest for he experimented with colour photography well before it came with in the reach of most amateur photographers or indeed before the populace at large became familiar with it in the cinema. There exist some colour transparencies, using the Duffay process, which date from 1938 (one is reproduced in "The Light of the Glens") and the great mystery is why there is not more colour work in the Collection. It does contain a very few colour prints but no transparencies. Yet this process became readily and inexpensively available in the 1950s when he was very active with his camera in and around the Clyde area. Let us be thankful that the black and white prints and negatives have survived.

The negatives were acquired by Dr. William Lind of The Ballast Trust where there they were catalogued and the richness of the photographic archive began to emerge. Without Bill Lind's initiative and his dedicated work and that of his staff it would not have been possible to produce this volume. So McDonald took a lot of photographs. So what? He did not just take pictures, he took high quality studies of his subjects with an excellent eye for composition as well as for detail. In a McDonald photograph we can take correct exposure and sharpness of focus for granted - even when the subject is in motion. The photographs of the complexities of the rigging and deck gear of the sailing ships not only show a desire to record detail for posterity but also encourage the viewer to peer into the corners and recesses in search of information. He could capture "atmosphere"; look at the picture of the puffer *Turk* that became the cover of his own book. The portraits of the river folk, the tug masters and the cabin boys, for example, capture the

The busy River in 1948. The 14,000 ton *Arawar* is being edged up-river by three tugs.

characters with humour and affection. They go a long way to explaining why he was always welcome on board.

With so many riches in the Collection it was difficult to know where to begin or where to end in trying to represent the photographs and do them justice in any publication. There is enough material for a dozen or so books. Fishing vessels and the East coast fishing ports, the ocean going liners, tugs, the last days of sail, puffers, the railways' steamers, cross-river ferries, the great shipping lines etc. could all have their histories comprehensively illustrated from Dan McDonald's pictures.

The unifying theme of this book is of course the River Clyde itself. He was born on the Clyde and he spent many hours on its banks. It was probably the dominating influence, outside family and work, in his life. It seemed fitting therefore to present this book as a visual history of the sixty years that he photographed the Clyde. Sadly therefore most of the fishing boat pictures, for example, had to be excluded. In compiling this volume a stern discipline had to be imposed - a picture had to relate to the Clyde to justify inclusion no matter what were the temptations offered by the quality or the historic interest of images from other airts.

What follows is intended to be a tribute to one of Glasgow's unsung heroes and to the River that he so obviously loved.

The Crinan Canal was an important link between the Clyde and the West Highlands for fishermen, puffermen and yachtsmen until the 1950s. A yacht has just come up through Dunardy Lock and passes Scottish Malt Distiller's puffer, *Pibroch*, on whose masthead the White Horse of its principle whisky brand can be clearly seen.

Pibroch 1923/100

A sight familiar to many Glaswegians; *sv Carrick*, moored at the Victoria Bridge in the heart of the City in the days when she was the clubhouse of the Royal Naval Volunteer Reserve. Launched at Sunderland as the wool clipper *City of Adelaide*, she took emigrants to Australia and brought back wool and wheat. She was acquired by the Royal Navy in 1893 and used as a training vessel at Greenock.

When her role as a clubhouse ended she came into the hands of some well-intentioned but inexperienced enthusiasts who managed to sink her. She was raised and removed to the Scottish Maritime Museum at Irvine where, in expert hands, a lengthy project to restore her to her nineteenth century state is underway.

sv Carrick 1864/790

The Last Days of Sail

Conventional wisdom has it that the opening of the Suez Canal in 1869 dealt the death blow to the supremacy of sailing ships in world-wide trade. The opening of the Canal reduced the distance from London to Bombay from 10,700 sea miles to only 6,300. Thus the steamship became less dependent on coaling stations and could devote more of its finite space to profit-making cargo than to the coal that was to be consumed in raising steam for propulsion.

How was it then that sailing ships could be regularly observed visiting the Clyde in the 1920s and 1930s? Were they still commercially viable or was some ultra-conservative or sentimental shipowner merely indulging himself? Pro-sail sentiment certainly existed but surely nobody could set their face against sixty years of technological and economic advance in the mercantile marine. Did sail still pay its way?

In truth it was the metallurgist rather than the civil engineer who signalled the beginning of the end for sail. When he produced high quality steel plate at low cost in the 1880s high pressure steam boilers became a practical reality. In 1887 a boiler capable of withstanding a steam pressure of 150 pounds per square inch, a considerable advance on the 60 pounds that could be achieved with wrought iron, was manufactured.

Five spars cross one of the masts of the *Madelaine Vinnen* and the photograph captures the lacework of the lines controlling this one mast's sails. This four-masted barque, built by Krupps at Kiel, had just discharged five and a half thousand tons of linseed at Glasgow.

Madelaine Vinnen 1892/3,400

When coupled to a triple expansion steam engine the coal consumption required to sustain long distance voyages virtually halved compared with the existing low pressure compound engine of the previous two decades. It was the skills of Bessemer, Siemens and a host of unsung boiler makers rather than the labours of M. de Lesseps that transformed commercial shipping. But this was twenty years after the opening of the Suez Canal.

Steamers were not dependent on fickle wind-power, were now more efficient and could carry more cargo than before. Surely now the sailing ship must disappear? In the twenty years after 1890 the number of foreign-going sailing vessels on the British register fell dramatically while the number and the tonnage of steam ships increased. Yet the

square riggers were still being built until World War I and earning their keep well afterwards. How had they managed to compete?

They competed by continuously improving. Their hull shapes developed radically in the 1860s. The bluff shape of the East Indiaman gave way to the sleek clipper. It was also an advantage that the copper sheathed composite hull of a sailing ship did not foul over with marine growths like the hull of the all metal steam ship. The square riggers could sail several knots faster than the steamers, given a fair wind, and that mattered on voyages to the other side of the world. What is more their masters knew how to find those fair winds.

In the period 1847-51, M. F. Maury of the United States Navy published the results of his statistical analyses of the winds and currents experienced on many voyages over many years. The charts and sailing directions that he produced gave ships' masters a ready reckoner of the oceans. A series of ocean guidelines were set out and favourable currents and winds, with their seasonal variations, could be found. Using Maury the 12,000 mile journey from Britain to Australia via the Cape of Good Hope was reduced from an average of one hundred and twenty days to around ninety. The distance from Britain to Australia via the Cape of Good Hope was only eight hundred and fifty miles longer than the voyage via Suez. With the knowledge of where to find the favourable Westerlies, sailing speeds of up to fourteen knots could be achieved. As a result the passage times were no longer than those of the steamers using the Canal.

From the 1860s through to the 1890s passage times from San Francisco to the U. K. round the Horn, West to East, were of the order of 90 to 100 days. It could take as little as 70 days from Greenock to Queensland and vessels often used this Eastern route to the West coast of America rather than spend weeks battling to windward against Westerly gales at Cape Horn. In one famous instance in 1896 two square riggers had totally different experiences on

The four masted barque, *Archibald Russell*, was the last deep sea sailing ship to be built on the Clyde. She was constructed at Scotts' Shipbuilding and Engineering Co., Greenock, for the Glasgow owner J. Hardie & Co. who operated her until 1922. Under the Finnish ownership of Erikson she won the annual grain race in 1929 with a passage from Melbourne to Queenstown (now Cobh) in 93 days.
Archibald Russell 1900/800

22

The Port Glasgow built *Parma*, drying her sails in the Kingston Dock in 1936, had just arrived with a cargo of wheat.

the Westerly and Easterly routes. *Fairport* took 176 days from Hamburg to San Francisco via the Horn and when she arrived found *Trafalgar* already there. The two ships had sighted each other at the Equator but *Trafalgar* had sailed to Sydney in 88 days and then taken 52 from Sydney to San Francisco, 140 days in total. Further she had spent 27 days in Australia discharging one cargo and loading another!

Clyde built clippers could be as fast as any. *Machrihanish* was constructed at the Port Glasgow yard of Robert Duncan in 1883 for Ardrossan owner Hugh Hogarth, who was later to build up a substantial fleet of steamers. This three-master took only 99 days from Portland, Oregon, to the Fastnet Rock in 1892. She carried a full cargo of that delicacy much favoured in the West of Scotland, tinned salmon. She would have been popular for more than just her speed on the voyage.

Even as its number declined at the end of the nineteenth century, the square rigger continued to develop. Steam winches were applied to the working of yards, sails and anchors and ton for ton the crew numbers were reduced by the order of twenty five percent. The introduction of steel masts and wire rigging reduced maintenance costs and with the acceptance of steel as a material for building hulls the sailing vessel became larger. The 2,000 ton deadweight square rigger of the 1890s had twice the cargo capacity of the typical ship of the 1860s. All of these changes helped sail resist the inevitable advance of steam but it had to fall back on a restricted range of specialised commodity trades. As a consequence the sailing ship continued to be the economic carrier of choice for Europe's export of coal and its import of the cheap bulk cargoes of India's jute, Australia's wool and grain, Chile's nitrates and California's wheat.

Is this Uncle Ned himself? Despite the Napoleonic pose, the figurehead of *Uncle Ned* has a resigned rather than an imperial expression. Perhaps his Dublin registration has given him a philosophical outlook on life.

Uncle Ned 1867/190

Two Glasgow shipowners, J. M. Campbell and Thomas Law, stayed loyal to sail and at the turn of the century were operating nearly thirty square riggers between them, mostly in the Australian grain trade. Both began to buy steamers around 1906 and Campbell sold his last sailer in 1911. Law did not part with his until 1919.

Few sailing vessels were built after World War I but until then a few owners continued to push up the deadweight size of the sailer to try to take advantage of the economies of scale. The largest sailing vessel built was the *France II* of 1911 which had a deadweight of 8,000 tons. She carried European coal to Tasmania via Good Hope and brought nickel ore back round the Horn. She survived a post-war stranding but the trade slump of the 1920s put paid to her.

The last sailing ship built on the Clyde was the *Archibald Russell*, launched from Scott's of Greenock in 1905. When she was captured on film in Glasgow in 1936 she was in the ownership of Captain Gustav Erikson of Mariehamn.

Gustav Erikson has an unique position in the history of the square rigged sailing ship. Born in Finland's Aland Islands he served under sail and after he went ashore in 1913 to become a shipowner he gradually built up a fleet of sailing ships by acquiring them second-hand. He restored their original names to them and re-registered them at his home port of Mariehamn. In the 1920s he had a fleet of seventeen, the oldest of which was the 1889 *Grace Harwar*. He managed to trade them profitably bringing Australian grain to Europe. Something of the experience of sailing in these ocean thoroughbreds is captured in Newby's book "The Last Grain Race".

The opening of the Panama Canal in 1914 had made the route from the Atlantic to the Pacific thousands of miles shorter by cutting out the need to round Cape Horn and the sailing ships could no longer compete on the trades to the West coast of the Americas. Some square riggers did use the Panama Canal but their transit costs were higher than the steamships since they had to be towed all the way.

In the 1930s it became more difficult for Erikson to make his square riggers break even and latterly he relied partly on volunteers to crew them for him. They manned his ships for the sake of the unique and disappearing adventure of sail. Thirteen of his vessels were still operating in 1939 and many of these plied their trade into Scotland. All of the ocean-going vessels shown here were Erikson's and without his vision and love of sail we would have been denied this glimpse of our maritime heritage. Only six survived World War II and a few are preserved today, laid up in various ports. They did not return to Glasgow and what we have here is a record of the last days of sail on the Clyde.

The three-masted topsail schooner, *Alert* had been built at Runcorn on the Mersey in 1885 and for half a century she plied various trades round the coast of the UK. Like their deep-sea sisters, few coastal sailing ships were built after 1900 and even fewer survived until after World War II. Here, recently discharged, she is lying in Glasgow's Kingston Dock in 1931.

Alert 1885/100

Harmony was originally built as a wooden sailing vessel, *Lorna*, by the Tay Shipbuilding Co. in Dundee. She was later converted to an auxiliary schooner to extend her life and usefulness for the coastal trade. Here she is, at nearly fifty years old, still working; her funnel seems to have been accommodated comfortably between the main and mizzen masts.

Harmony 1876/400

The *M.A. James* is the subject of some speculation on the part of the three "wee Glesga laddies" as she lies peacefully in a quiet corner of the Kingston dock in 1928. One may speculate, on the evidence of the empty basin on the hatch, that the crewman reading in the shade of the mizzen, has just hung out the washing on the port shrouds.

M.A. James 1900/120

The anchor windlass of the *Alert* speaks to us of an age of lower technology. The wooden frame and drums and the simple metal gears and brakes suggest something of the hard manual labour of weighing anchor on coastal schooners of this era. This picture was taken when she was 50 years old, so little had been done to modernise the arrangement.

Alert 1885/100

Crewmen, discussing a point, gathered round the sheet winch on the schooner *My Lady of Plymouth*. Such mechanical aids would have been needed to haul up sails or to sheet them in when full of wind. Working cargo on these ships would not have been easy given the relatively small hatches.

My Lady of Plymouth 1889/100

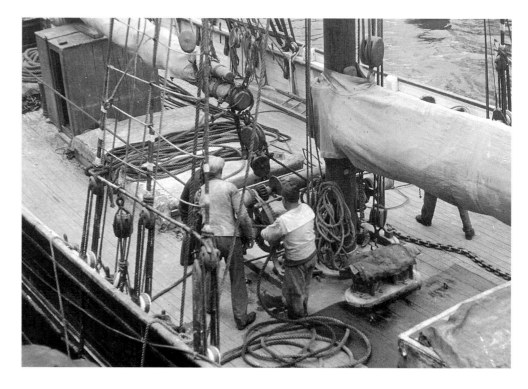

The three-master, *Grace Harwar*, was another of the square riggers rescued by Gustav Erikson. He did not have a theme or sequence of related names for his ships. When he bought them he simply restored the names under which they had been launched.

She had a reputation for speed having made a passage to London from Talcahuano in Chile in 87 days. Her bowsprit was carried away in a collision and yet she arrived in Falmouth, even with this disability, with nitrate from Iquique (much further north than Talcahuano) in 114 days.

Grace Harwar 1889/1,870

L'Avenir was originally a sail training ship but like the others in the Erikson fleet she became a grain racer, frequently competing against the *Archibald Russell*. The starboard anchor has been brought in board to allow painting of the hull. Obviously the 1934 Safety Inspector, if such had existed then, took a more relaxed view about the wearing of lifejackets and the rigging of safety nets than would his modern day counterpart.

L'Avenir 1908/2,700

The *Clackmananshire* lies in the Gareloch in October 1922 waiting her turn at the breaker's berth. She was one of Thomas Law's "shires" and her last cargo to the Clyde had been maize from Port Natal. Law had taken delivery of her from Russell & Co. of Greenock in 1884 and he stuck loyally to sail through the turn of the century. From this time on it was only the dedicatees like Erikson who refused to espouse steam. This picture poignantly recalls the last days of many other square riggers.

Clackmananshire 1884/1,580

L'Avenir has her course, upper and lower topsail yards tilted to starboard. This is so that they will not interfere with the operating of the boom of the shoreside cranes on the port side as they discharge the vessel. This was standard practice on sailing ships.

L'Avenir 1908/2,700

Olivebank came into Erikson's fleet in 1924 and so found her way into the Australian grain trade. This four masted steel barque was a product of the Mackie and Thomson yard at Govan. The sweep of her deck is well captured here.

She became the victim of a mine soon after the outbreak of war in September 1939, three years after this picture was taken. She went down, East of Scarborough, at the southern edge of the Dogger Bank, with the loss of fourteen of her crew of twenty-one.

Her wreck has been discovered as recently as 1997. Among the artifacts recovered was her chronometer, stopped at 15.30 hrs., presumably the time of her sinking.

Olivebank 1892/2,600

The figurehead of the *M.A. James* looks wistfully out from the complexity of the bowsprit rigging.

The practice of fixing emblems to the bows of ships, probably dates from Greek and Roman times when an acrostolium, a symbolic ornament, often in the shape of a shield or helmet, was incorporated in the prow of a galley. The superstition was that this warded off evil spirits or appeased the gods of the sea.

Carvings of women were the most popular types of figurehead in the nineteenth century. They usually had one if not both breasts uncovered, reflecting the seaman's superstition that, while women were unlucky, an unclad woman had the power to calm a storm at sea. (Even if at the same time she was raising one in the heart of her male beholder.) The Victorian need for modesty has the young lady on the *M.A. James* well covered.

In both merchant and war ships, as iron and then steel replaced wood and steam ousted sail, the figurehead began to disappear. There was no convenient bowsprit to fit the figure under and the straight metal stem of the steamer was an unsympathetic medium in which to produce works of art. Nevertheless the tradition has not died completely and a few modern shipowners still adorn the bows of their vessels with decorative emblems.

M.A. James 1900/120

Great Britain was not the only maritime power to practise gunboat diplomacy. Here we have an American gunboat *Ranger* in the Clyde! The 1875 auxiliary barquentine was converted to the Massachussetts Naval Training School and renamed *Nantucket*. In that guise she visited the Clyde in 1928. The crewman is unmistakenly "American".

Nantucket 1875

Survivors

The "P" Line of Hamburg owned many sailing vessels and at least two survive to this day. *Padua*, whose ornate steering gear box is seen here, became the U.S.S.R. training ship Kruzenstern. *Passat* (not shown here) is preserved at Lubeck.

Moshulu, whose bowsprit is shown here, was constructed at Port Glasgow by Hamiltons in 1904, and is now a floating restaurant at Philadelphia.

Pommern, seen under tug escort in the Clyde, lies at Mariehamn as a tribute to Gustav Erikson.

Padua 1926/3,100
Moshulu 1904/3,100
Pommern 1903/2,400

This picture was not taken on the Clyde, for the *Cutty Sark* now lies at Greenwich but Dan McDonald could not resist going to see what is probably the Clyde's most famous sailing ship. Ironic, is it not, that this Scottish ship is preserved in England while the English built clipper, *Carrick* or *City of Adelaide*, is to be preserved in Scotland?

She belongs to the last era of British clippers and was designed for the China tea races. However, she spent most of her working life in the Australian wool trade. In 1872 she arrived in the Thames a week behind *Thermopylae* after they had raced from Shanghai with their "first-of-the-season" tea cargoes; she had lost her rudder when comfortably in the lead and spent six days, at sea, rigging a replacement.

She was completed by Denny of Dumbarton in 1869 after the yard which laid her down went into liquidation. Of composite construction (wooden hull on iron frames) her top speed was reckoned to be 17.5 knots. Her best run in a 24 hour period was 363 miles - an average speed of just over 15 knots.

Cutty Sark 1869/920

When grain sacks were discharged from the sailing ships, horse transport and manual labour were still the order of the day in the Glasgow docks of the 1920s. This is a scene that would have changed little in a hundred years.

Lines of Yards

It is July 1964 and the cranes at Harland and Wolff are motionless and the berths are empty. In October 1963 the yard had been put on "care and maintenance" - a euphemism for closure. Two years later the land was sold for housing.

There was a time when the Clyde was lined with shipbuilding yards - certainly for most of the period that Dan McDonald was taking his photographs.

The hoary old saw that "The Clyde made Glasgow and Glasgow made the Clyde", encapsulating the inter-dependence of the city and its river, was never more true than it was applied to the relationship between the companies which built the ships and the companies that owned and operated them.

It is not at all unusual in the great shipbuilding centres of the world for mutually dependent industries to grow up. Many factors contribute to this, not least the existence of an industrial infrastructure close to a natural port. Glasgow and the Clyde had many of these attributes in abundance.

Natural resources in the form of coal and ironstone, an imperfect but correctable waterway and an established trading centre were all present in West and Central Scotland from the 1840s onwards.

Long before the management sciences coined the jargon "vertical integration" the shipbuilder and the owner saw the inherent logic of investing in each others' businesses. It made sense either to own the means of manufacturing the ship that created the wealth or to have a share in the profits made by the ship that you had built. That way the owner needed the yard and the yard needed the owner.

Samuel Cunard, who established what was later to become one of the world's most famous transatlantic liner companies in 1839, did so by securing a contract to carry mail from Liverpool to Nova Scotia. He built his first four ships on the Clyde, with Robert Napier who was renowned as a manufacturer of steam engines. (Napier let him have them cheaply with a view to securing future contracts.) With Napier's help he had raised £82,500, mostly from a group of Glaswegian businessmen, to set up the enterprise. The Cunard Line's relationship with the Clyde was to continue till the launching of the *Queen Elizabeth 2* in 1967.

Another famous Glasgow shipping company, Paddy Henderson (1834 to 1961), was backed in its most famous enterprise, the Irrawaddy Flotilla Company Ltd., first registered in 1876, by the shipbuilding company of William Denny and Bros. of Dumbarton. At its peak the Flotilla was the biggest inland shipping company in the world with over six hundred vessels, most of them built by Denny. Captain Tom Henderson had originally traded sailing ships to New Zealand and found it useful to call at Burma on the return leg to load cargoes of rice and teak.

Also established in 1876 was the Clan Line. Its first three steamers were built and partly owned by Alexander Stephen & Sons Ltd. of Linthouse. The "clan" name was

carried by two hundred and fifty-two ships, half of which were launched on the Clyde. Of these, sixty-seven came from the Greenock Dockyard Co., which Clan partly and eventually completely, owned. They also had their own ship repair yard at Finnieston from 1890 until 1971.

Anchor Line, which ran Glasgow to New York passenger and cargo services, had as one of its founding shareholders, the Henderson family. They bought out Tod and McGregor's shipyard at Meadowside, renamed it D. & W. Henderson & Co. Ltd., and naturally produced most of Anchor Line's liners.

This pattern was repeated many times over. Shipbuilder Lithgows Ltd. partly owned the vessels of Lyle Shipping, (1903 to 1987), the Glasgow based tramping company. Barclay Curle (originally established in 1845 at Stobcross) held equity in the Donaldson line. From further afield, Alfred Holt (Ocean Steamship Co.) and China Navigation had cross-shareholdings with Scotts of Greenock, the latter ordering ninety-six ships from Scotts. Charles Connell & Co. Ltd. of Scotstoun owned shares in the Edinburgh based Ben Line and coincidentally produced thirty vessels for them.

Blue Star Line's Bremen built *Canberra Star* is dramatically highlighted by a shaft of sunlight as she lies in King George V Dock. With his sure eye for a photographic image Dan McDonald has produced a dramatic shot.

Canberra Star 1956/8,300

What could go up could also come down. Anchor Line went into liquidation in 1935 but the name was kept alive by Runciman (London) Ltd. who picked up the pieces. The liquidation brought down the Govan yard of Fairfields (Fairfield Shipbuilding and Engineering Co. Ltd.), which was rescued by two of the Lithgow brothers.

There was one shipping line that was above all this commercial in-breeding - the Grey Funnel Line, otherwise known as the Royal Navy.

Constructing warships had traditionally been the preserve of the Naval Dockyards, like Chatham, but with the coming of steam where else would the Admiralty look for expertise but the Clyde and Robert Napier? He was more famous as a manufacturer of engines than hulls but he had the distinction of building the second ironclad, HMS *Black Prince*, in 1862. Napier's Govan yard was taken over by Beardmore in 1900 (the great man had died in 1876) and in the pre-1914 period there were five major companies on the Clyde which were regarded as 'Admiralty' yards. These were the aforementioned Beardmore, Fairfield, Brown, Yarrow and Scotts of Greenock. (Brown of Sheffield and Beardmore of Parkhead were really iron and steel makers who bought into Clyde shipbuilding to secure outlets for their products.) In fact at the outbreak of the 1914-18 hostilities Fairfield, Beardmore and Brown were "taken over" by the Royal Navy and not allowed to build merchantmen.

Turning out warships was not just the monopoly of these yards during the two World Wars or the inter-war years, and many other Clyde yards contributed their share of specialised war tonnage. But from these large yards came many of the Navy's famous names like *Valiant*, *Hood*, *Duke of York* and the last British battleship of all, *Vanguard*. Big surface ships became obsolete with the development of the nuclear submarine as the primary Naval weapon and four of the big five names are no more. The Clyde continues to meet the Navy's much changed late twentieth century needs through the continued existence of Yarrow & Co. which

has a tradition, going back over a hundred years, of producing high speed Naval craft.

Just prior to World War I there were thirty-eight yards on the Clyde from Glasgow to Greenock. Over one hundred thousand people were directly employed and two hundred and thirty ships were launched. Today there are three shipbuilding yards in full-time operation. The story of this decline has been well chronicled and many reasons have been advanced to explain it. (This is not the place to debate the pros and cons of nationalisation of the shipbuilding industry in 1977 or to retell the saga of Upper Clyde Shipbuilders of a decade earlier.) The 1960s brought the containerisation revolution in cargo handling and a demand for ever larger and deeper drafted ships than the Clyde with its physical limitations could satisfy. Among the political, economic and technological factors advanced for the demise of shipbuilding on the Clyde the conservatism of management and the intransigence of labour are at the top of most people's lists. But the inter-dependence of the shipowner and the shipbuilder has not been given the attention it deserves.

The owner lost his markets. The political independence of Burma, for example, wiped out the Irrawaddy Flotilla Company. Containerisation, where one container ship could do the work of six general cargo vessels, soon made traditional services, like Donaldson's South America trade, uneconomic. So the shipowner bought fewer ships or even went out of business. The loss of these ship operating profits affected the prosperity of the yards which held his shares. Then of course the yard suffered from the lack of orders and its fragile profitability declined further. Holding shares in an unprofitable shipbuilding concern inevitably hastened the demise of the troubled ship owner. And so the spiral went accelerating downwards. Vertical integration had become vertical disintegration. The 1960s became the decade of yard closures on the Clyde and of the disappearance of many of its famous "lines".

Carinthia was constructed at Brown's at Clydebank for Cunard to run between Greenock and Liverpool to Halifax. She came into service exactly when the jet aircraft was beginning to get the upper hand on the transatlantic passenger trade and she was in commission for only ten years. She could carry up to eight hundred and fifty passengers and about six hundred tons of cargo but having to lay up in the winter when the St Lawrence was frozen did not help the economics of her operations.

Carinthia 1956/21,900

The cargo-liner *Glenfinlas* was launched from John Brown's West Yard at Clydebank in 1966 for the Ocean Transport and Trading Group. By this time the East Yard, in an effort to meet the demands of the times, had gone over to the production of jack-up rigs for North Sea oil production. The remaining shipbuilding activities were to be absorbed into Upper Clyde Shipbuilders in 1968 and by 1973 the last ship from this famous yard had gone down the slips.

Glenfinlas 1966/12,000

Canadian Pacific Steamship's *Empress of Britain (II)* makes her stately way down the River. Little wonder she earned the soubriquet "Queen of the Pacific".

A founding shareholder of this company, Sir William G. Pearce, was the Chairman of Fairfields yard and that is where this empress was built. Following John Elder's death his Govan shipyard business was reconstituted financially. It was bought over by the Pearce family in 1886 and renamed the Fairfield Shipbuilding & Engineering Co. Ltd. The continuity of ship production at this location is maintained to this day by Kvaerner Govan Ltd.

Empress of Britain was to have the sad distinction of being the largest liner sunk in World War II. She was bombed in 1940 while carrying troops and while under tow to safety was torpedoed by U-32.

Empress of Britain 1930/42,300

Emigration. The *Montlaurier* outward bound for Montreal. The "Glasgow Herald" of the 24th of September 1924 reported "Two sailings took place from the Clyde on Saturday with passengers for the USA and Canada. The CPR liner *Montlaurier* and the White Star liner *Megantic* arrived at the Tail of the Bank during the morning from Liverpool and several special trains were necessary to convey passengers from Glasgow to Princes Pier. The emigrants were afterwards taken out by tenders to the vessels waiting at the anchorage. Both liners sailed in the afternoon and their complement was about 2,500 passengers."

Montlaurier 1907/17,300

This Canadian Pacific ship was a kaiserin rather than an empress, having been built in Germany in 1914 as the *Tirpitz*. She was handed over to the British as part of the War reparations and renamed *Empress of Australia (I)* in 1922. She is on her way to Fairfields in 1926 to be re-engined with turbines.

The Canadian Pacific Railway Company had got into shipping in 1884 to serve the Great Lakes and the Pacific Northwest coast to complement its transcontinental train routes. From Vancouver it traded to the Far East and eventually owned ships to do so. Logic dictated that if they looked West from Vancouver then they should also look East from Montreal. If the mail could cross the Atlantic in Canadian Pacific Railway ships then it could get from Hong Kong to London via Canada faster than it would on P. & O. ships using the Suez Canal.

Empress of Australia 1914/21,500

In 1915 Canadian Pacific took over the Allan Line's service from the Clyde to Canada with which it had been initially in competition and the *Empress of Canada (I)* was destined for the route. In 1903 The Canadian Pacific Railway had acquired the North Atlantic route interests of Elder, Dempster & Co. which brought them into this trade for the first time. They built their first ships for the Glasgow/Liverpool/Quebec route, the *Empress of Britain (I)* and the *Empress of Ireland (I)*, at Fairfields in 1906. Thereby, they coincidentally forged another link with the past of the Elder family.

Empress of Canada 1922/21,500

The *Uganda* survives today in the specialist educational cruise market but she was originally built by Barclay Curle for the British India Steam Navigation Company. British India, at the time of its amalgamation in 1914 with P. & O., had been one of Britain's largest shipowners. Its East African cargo and passenger trade, for which the *Uganda* was designed, was effectively killed off by the closure of the Suez Canal in 1967.

In the Falklands war *Uganda* became a N.O.S.H. (Naval Ocean-going Surgical Hospital) and treated British and Argentinians alike. Thereafter she reverted to cruising.

Uganda 1952/16,900

Anchor Line's mainstay was the Glasgow to New York emigrant trade. In the hundred years up to the outbreak of the 1939 hostilities over two million Scots emigrated to Canada and America. Companies like Anchor prospered in providing this service.

The Line was set up in 1856 and the Henderson family, who went on to operate the Meadowside yard of D. & W. Henderson Ltd., were major shareholders. Up to 1935 Anchor Line built many of their fleet at Hendersons.

City of Rome was a transitional ship and looks more like a sailing ship than a steamer with her bowsprit and masts. She had accommodation for one thousand passengers but was soon pushed off her Liverpool to New York run by faster ships, like the Cunarders. (The ship was broken up in 1903 and this a photograph of a photograph that Dan McDonald took much later.)

City of Rome 1881/8,400

The Fairfield built *Athenia* is notorious for being the first ship torpedoed after the outbreak of World War II - seven hours after the official declaration on September 3rd 1939. One hundred and twelve of her passengers and crew died.

The same U-boat commander was forced to surface two years later after sinking another Anchor-Donaldson ship and this led to the discovery of an Enigma machine and subsequently to the breaking of the U-boat communication codes.

Athenia 1923/13,500

Donaldson Line's third *Letitia* was to be their last newbuilding for within six years the company went into voluntary liquidation. They suffered badly, especially on the South American trades, from the competition from containerisation. Though well designed and equipped she has evolved from the traditional cargo/passenger liner. One containership could do the work of six of her kind.

The original company had been established in 1858 by two Donaldson brothers who traded sailing ships to the River Plate. They acquired their first steamer from Barclay Curle in 1870 and soon began regular runs to Canada. This business took them into the mass emigration market and led eventually to their linking up with Cunard to form the Anchor-Donaldson Line in 1916.

Letitia 1961/4,700

This Linthouse built vessel was the fourth Anchor Line ship to carry the name *Caledonia*. Anchor Line was bought by Cunard in 1911 so that the latter could get into the cheap end of the transatlantic trade. The restrictions placed on immigration numbers by the United States in the wake of the Great Depression virtually killed off the trade and Anchor went into liquidation in 1935.

Caledonia was placed on this emigrant trade in the inter-war years and was transferred to Donaldson-Atlantic Line after the Anchor collapse. She was converted to that curious breed, the Armed Merchant Cruiser, in 1939 and renamed HMS *Scotstoun*. Such ships may have been large enough to make gun platforms but their lack of armour meant that they were no match for a real warship if they encountered one. She was sunk by a U-boat while on patrol in the Atlantic in 1940.

Caledonia 1925/17,000

On a June day in 1924 HMS *Malaya* lies at anchor in Lamlash Bay. She lies alongside three other Queen Elizabeth type battleships. They were the Clydebuilt *Barham* and *Valiant* and the *Warspite*. (*Warspite* was built at Devonport and engined by Fairfields.) With eight fifteen inch guns, twelve six inch guns and top speed of 25 knots they represented the latest thinking in the British World War I naval strategy. *Warspite* had been at the battle of Jutland in 1916 and survived to be at Cape Matapan in the 1941 victory over an Italian fleet. Indeed, all five fought in World War II and only *Barham* was lost - torpedoed in the Mediterranean in 1941.

HMS *Malaya* 1916/33,000

Laid up in the Gareloch in 1950, with covers on the guns that finished off the *Bismarck*, the *King George V* still looks to be in good trim. She was the flagship of the Commander-in-Chief of the Home Fleet in 1941 when she set out to intercept the German battleship which had sunk the *Hood*. She was broken up at Dalmuir in 1958.

HMS *King George V* 1939/35,000

The Clyde's and the Royal Navy's last battleship was built at Brown's at Clydebank in 1944. *Vanguard* came back to the Clyde to be broken up in 1960 without ever having fired a shot in anger. Even when she was laid down in 1941 she was an obsolete concept - made so by the torpedo and the aerial bomb. From this point on the aircraft carrier and the submarine were to be the capital ships of the world's navies.

HMS *Vanguard* 1944/44,500

HMS *Clyde* carries the River's name and while she is not one of the great ships of war for which the Clyde was famous, she is none the less an elegant example of the Royal Navy's wooden-hulled coastal minesweepers. Seen here in 1957, she was used as a training ship for the Clyde's Royal Naval Volunteer Reserve, having been renamed from HMS *Amerton*.

HMS *Clyde* 1945/420

The Clyde's warship building tradition is still carried on today by Yarrow's yard at Scotstoun. (They first produced torpedo boat destroyers for the Royal Navy in 1911.) Between 1975 and 1978 five Type 21 gas turbine frigates were built. One of these was HMS *Ardent*, *F184* which became a casualty of the Falklands War. The yard has gone on to produce both the Type 22 and the Type 23 frigates. The latter class's electronically controlled missiles are a far cry from the 15 inch guns fitted to the battleships of old.

HMS *Ardent* 1977/3,200

By the end of World War II, during which she had been engaged in convoy protection and bombardment duties, *Renown* was the last survivor of the previous war's ill-fated battle-cruiser concept. Launched from Fairfield's in 1916 she lies in the Gareloch waiting to be broken up.

As a class, the battle-cruisers were given large guns but their high speed, to allow them to carry out reconnaissance duties, was achieved at the expense of armour. It was a dangerous misconception to treat them as battleships because of their name and armament. With their light deck armour they were vulnerable to plunging fire penetrating and exploding their magazines. The loss of *Hood* when she met a real battleship, the *Bismarck*, was a sad reminder of this fact. *Indefatigable*, another battle-cruiser had been lost at Jutland in 1916 in the same way but the lesson was not learned.

HMS *Renown* 1916/32,000

The continuity of design in the Blue Funnel technical department is evident in this view of two Holt's ships at their usual berth in King George V Dock. The *Melampus* was one of six sister ships ordered in the late 1950s as the final part of the post-war replacement programme which took the Blue Flue fleet up to a total of sixty vessels. (The ship astern of her could be another "M" but the name is not clear.) This was the high water mark for this fleet which was soon to be overtaken by dramatic technical and socio-economic changes in the business of shipping. *Melampus* was "lost" in the Six Day War closure of the Suez Canal but in any event she and her sisters were proved obsolete by events.

By 1973 most of Ocean's trades had been transferred to OCL and in 1986 it got out of shipping completely by selling its share in the consortium.

Melampus 1960/8,500

Under tow to the usual Blue Funnel berth in King George V Dock *Adrastus* is seen here passing the Stone Manganese factory. Famous for its non-ferrous products and for its machining capabilities many a Glasgow ship owner was grateful to it for the repair of chipped and bent propeller blades.

It was from Scotts' yard at Greenock that the Ocean Steam Ship Company, the "proper" version of the Holts/Blue Flue name, had ordered its first three steam ships, *Agamemnon*, *Ajax* and *Achilles*, to be driven by compound steam engines. They opened up Holt's new route to China. The Liverpool company came back to Scotts' over eighty times for their new ships after that first experience in 1865.

The picture dates from 1963. Two years later Ocean had gone into a containerisation consortium, Overseas Containers Ltd., and the days of the likes of the *Adrastus* were numbered.

Adrastus 1953/7,900

The main interest in this picture of the *Geologist* is the fact that she is being loaded by a floating crane. In fact, her cargo was locomotives for South Africa from the North British Locomotive Company at Springburn. This world famous manufacturer of steam engines was formed in 1903 by the amalgamation of three local companies. The need to load these heavy engines onto ships brought about the building of a Clydeside landmark. A steam crane of one hundred and thirty tons lifting capacity was placed at Stobcross Quay in 1895. This was replaced in 1932 by the one hundred and seventy-five ton crane at Finnieston which is still to be seen on the north bank. North British ceased production in 1962, one hundred and ten years after the first locomotive was exported from the Glasgow docks.

Geologist 1914/6,200

Clan Lamont was built at the Greenock Dockyard Co. Ltd. which Clan Line's owners, Cayzer Irvine & Co., had bought after the 1914-18 War. At any one time anything up to 70% of the yard's capacity was devoted to producing ships for Clan Line. Such interdependence was a boon in prosperous times and an albatross at the bottom of the trade cycle. Clan Lamont served as HMS Ardpatrick in World War II and carried part of the United States Army onto Juno Beach in the Normandy landings of 1944.

Clan Lamont 1939/7,300

Clan Line always had a particularly strong association with the Clyde. During its life of just over a century more than half of its ships were launched from Clydeside yards. It was set up in 1878 with the financial help of Stephens' yard who produced their first three steamers. Its principal services were to India and South Africa. Its ships were frequent users of the Suez Canal where the charges were levied on deck area (as a measure of cargo-carrying capacity) and this led to the curious money-saving design known as the "turret ship". Clan Chattan was one such and the bow-on shot demonstrates the odd result - the body of the ship flares out from the narrow deck in an attempt to achieve a large hold capacity from a minimum deck surface. The "turrets" did not have a good reputation for stability and a few capsized in unexpected circumstances. The design was dropped before the 1914-18 War.

Clan Chattan 1902/3,900

Clan Forbes had a very distinguished record in the 1939 - 1946 conflict and survived some remarkable scrapes. She was bombed while lying at Tilbury in 1940 and took part in the convoys to Malta which brought badly needed supplies to that beleaguered island.

She was one of four, the others being Fraser, Ferguson and Menzies, that were launched from the Greenock Dockyard in 1938.

Clan Forbes 1938/7,500

Clan Line's first ship was called Clan Alpine. The Clan Alpine pictured here was the two hundred and fiftieth and last ship of the fleet. She was sold in 1981 when the line effectively ceased to operate as a separate entity. Like other cargo liner companies Clan's business was undermined by the loss of Imperial Preference and the dramatic changes that the 1960s and 1970s had brought to cargo handling techniques. Previously they had consolidated what remained of their trade into a UK based container group, Overseas Containers Ltd. Clan's other main link to the Clyde was severed in 1971 when they closed their repair facility at Finnieston.

Clan Alpine 1966/8,700

Baron Forbes, here seen passing the Govan Graving Docks, is a typical example of First World War ship design. She was built in Hamburg in 1915 and became a war prize of the British Government in 1919. Hogarth bought her in 1922 and she served them well for a further thirty-one years. She was deployed particularly on the company's trade to Spain and Portugal whence she returned with cargoes of iron pyrites for the Lanarkshire steel makers.

Hugh Hogarth, who had gone into business as a ships chandler in Ardrossan in the 1860s, bought his first steamship, *Baron Ardrossan*, in 1881. He had built up one of the largest tramping fleets in the United Kingdom by the outbreak of the 1939 War. The "Barons" always flew the Saltire at the masthead and a large number of them came from the Ayrshire Dockyard Company.

Baron Forbes 1915/3,100

The temporary repairs to the badly damaged *Baron Vernon* are clearly visible as she is towed into dock in 1924. She had collided with the much larger *Metagama* at Langbank the previous year and her master, realising she was in a sinking condition and not wanting to block the channel, ran her aground. There she had rested, subject to wind and tide for nearly a year. She was sold soon after this shot was taken. The previous *Baron Vernon*, built at Dumbarton in 1912, had been torpedoed in 1916. The 1929 new-building from Henderson's yard, which also carried this name, became a victim of U604 in 1942. Not a lucky title! While Hogarth often re-used names (as many as six times) there was never another *Vernon* after 1942.

Baron Vernon 1922/2,600

The cupola of the Clyde Navigation Trust's building on the North bank, a landmark of the upper River, serves as backdrop to the Highlander on the bowsprit of the *Kinloch*.

"Paddy Henderson" was a famous name on the Clyde, but it was even more famous in Dumbarton and Rangoon. The founding father of the Henderson family business only ever signed himself "Patrick" but as is the way in the West of Scotland this was shortened to "Paddy" and it stuck. The family had owned sailing ships from the 1820s to the 1880s and traded mainly to New Zealand. In search of return cargoes they began to call at Burma to load rice and teak. In 1874 they became the British and Burmese Steam Navigation Co.

Like most of the Henderson ships the *Kemmendine* was built at Denny of Dumbarton. She operated as a cargo/passenger liner for the Glasgow to Rangoon run and on such a voyage in 1940 she was lost to enemy action. The company lost six of its thirteen ships in World War II.

Kemmendine 1924/7,800

The Glasgow to Rangoon service re-opened in 1948 with four Denny-built ships but with the nationalisation of the Irrawaddy Flotilla in that same year the Paddy Henderson influence in the area waned. The British and Burmese company was taken over by Elder Dempster in 1952 and vessels such as the *Donga* were switched to their West African Trade.

Donga 1960/6,600

Pegu was a favoured name in Paddy Henderson. It was used for four ships between 1889 and 1961. Pegu is upstream from Rangoon on the Irrawaddy where the Irrawaddy Flotilla Company Ltd. had the world's largest inland shipping fleet. When the company was registered in 1876 Denny of Dumbarton backed it and naturally built the lion's share of its shallow drafted ships and barges. The Flotilla operated under the Henderson house flag and had a distinguishing red band on its black funnel. When Burma was invaded in 1942 five hundred and fifty of the company's six hundred and fifty craft were scuppered rather than let them fall into enemy hands. In 1948 Burma became independent and it nationalised the Flotilla Company which was formally liquidated in 1950. The British and Burmese Steam Navigation Co.'s last newbuilding was this *Pegu*.

Pegu 1961/5,800

The fate of those who were victims of the torpedoing of the *City of Cairo* in 1942 was one of the most harrowing of World War II. Her planned voyage from India via South Africa and Brazil to the UK, illustrates well the Far East trading pattern of the Ellerman ships. The fact that she was carrying passengers is a reminder that this was a typical between-the-Wars mixed cargo and passenger service.

The survivors endured a lengthy voyage in an open boat in the South Atlantic only to be picked up by a German ship. She was scuttled when she came under attack and those on board took to the life rafts. They were rescued again - by a U-boat. After a difficult under water passage, which included being depth-charged, the survivors of the *City of Cairo* became prisoners of war for the duration of the hostilities.

City of Cairo 1915/7,700

Barclay Curle's Whiteinch yard, after years of building sailing ships for City Line, produced this well-known Glasgow company's first steamship in 1870. It was a relationship that was to last for over a century and was not disturbed by the acquisition of City Line by the financier J.R. Ellerman in 1901. The line, which was generally referred to as "Ellerman's City Line", became part of a larger group of companies, but continued in its established passenger and cargo services to India under its distinctive orange white and black banded funnel. *The City of Lille* was the first diesel ship ordered by the company and so Barclay's had produced another first for City Line.

City of Lille 1928/6,600

Belfast-built specifically for the expanding cargo and passenger trade to India, the *City of London*, was for many years the largest and fastest ship in the City fleet. She is seen here in 1946 looking a little tired in her wartime grey. As an Armed Merchant Cruiser she had patrolled the South China Sea in the 1914-18 conflict and later distinguished herself as a troop carrier when she evacuated army personnel to Alexandria after the fall of Crete in 1941. Ellerman's lost eighty-three ships in World War II so this *London* was unique in surviving both conflicts. Sadly, worn out, she is on her way to the breakers at Dalmuir.

City of London 1907/9,000

The third and last *City of London*, was built at Upper Clyde Shipbuilders in 1970 and was one of the last cargo liners to be designed by Ellermans. The political independence of India and Pakistan and their desire to be mercantile nations in their own right, added to the changes wrought by containerships and bulk carriers made this type of ship obsolete. Ellermans did participate in one of the British container-ship consortia but the Ellerman company, as such, was sold in 1983 after a period of heavy loss-making.

City of London 1970/7,100

This group of eight are applying the final cosmetic cover to a damaged bow in No.3 Graving Dock. Or they would be if the one coming up the ladder with the "pent" would get a move on! (The *Malabar* was produced by Barclay Curle in 1925 for Australian owners and distinguished herself by hitting Weymss Bay pier on her trials.)

Below - the last of the line, this bulk carrier named *Hamlet*, appropriately enough for Danish owners, rests on the stocks prior to her launch. She was the last ship to be completed at the famous Barclay Curle yard. Robert Barclay and Robert Curle had gone into partnership in 1845 and moved their ship-building enterprise to the Clydeholm yard at Whiteinch ten years later.

Hamlet 1967/29,300

The Granary at Meadowside is one of the River's great landmarks - even today when it lies unused. The Clyde Navigation Trust began to build this complex in 1911 for the storage of Canadian grain which was imported for the local whisky distillers. (The site had previously been the stadium of Glasgow's greatest football team - Partick Thistle.) It was extended in 1937 after which it laid claim to be the largest brick structure in Europe. With the corporate takeovers and rationalisation of the whisky trade's distilling capacity the Granary was used less and less and finally closed in 1995.

In 1962, for the 150th anniversary of the first trip of the *Comet*, a full scale working replica of Henry Bell's vessel was built by the apprentices at Lithgows. She was shown widely around the Clyde and in the summer she ran on the original route from Bridge Wharf to the Gareloch via Greenock and Helensburgh, for the delectation of the City dwellers. A group are here caught giving the ship the once over. The old chap in the bunnet does not seem to be madly enthusiastic about parting with ten shillings for a trip. The youngster is more interested in the photographer than the intricacies of early steam engines. Thirty-six years on, where is that boy now?

Doon the Watter

The *Isle of Arran* operated for the Buchanan and the Williamson-Buchanan fleets from Glasgow to Bute rather than to the island of her name. She was the last ship to come down the slips at Seath's yard at Rutherglen.

Isle of Arran 1892/310

The "Glasgow Herald" of the 17th of September 1900 reported:

"The Caledonian Railway paddle steamer *Duchess of Rothesay* collided with the North British Railway steamer *Kenilworth* as they attempted to out run each other on service from Rothesay to Dunoon."

The situation had obviously changed little in forty years as the same organ in September 1861 had commented on the cut-throat competition among private steamer operators which had led to two captains appearing in court charged with "culpable and reckless navigation" in a race to be first at Kilcreggan pier.

Competition between companies on the Clyde had been fierce from its very earliest days. It was fed by the ambitions of the new and burgeoning railways who were determined to provide through services to all parts of the Clyde estuary for the Victorian traveller. They also had their eyes on the lucrative holiday and leisure excursion trade which was to become part of Clydeside lore and was to be known as going "doon the watter".

The Caledonian Railway opened up a railhead at Weymss Bay in 1865 and built its own pier at Greenock in 1884 to compete with the Glasgow and South Western Railway who had already established themselves there. The North British Railway Company, having previously operated from Helensburgh from 1865 when it acquired the Edinburgh and Glasgow Railway Company, used Craigendorran, on the North bank, as its "port" from 1882 onwards.

This is the North British Railway's *Kenilworth* that struck the *Duchess of Rothesay* in a race to berth first at Dunoon pier. It would appear that everything on this ship was done in a hurry. No one had time before she sailed to remove the canvass fixed on her lum. This cover would have been put in place to stop the black paint applied to the top of her funnel from splashing down on to the red below.

Kenilworth 1898/330

In advance of most of this activity, and before they considered becoming shipowners in their own right, the railways had formed operating agreements with a variety of long established private steamship owners, such as Buchanan and Williamson, and chartered their ships to operate as sea-going extensions to the timetables of their trains. (As early as 1841 the Glasgow Paisley and Greenock Railway had "sailed with" the Bute Steam Packet Co. to Rothesay.) It became a matter of honour to offer the fastest time from the centre of Glasgow to, say, Brodick. This meant not only synchronising the steamer's departure with the train's arrival but it put some emphasis on the speed and comfort of the ship. It also meant not being squeamish about cutting out the opposition in the race to get a berth at a pier.

From 1865 onwards, when the North British Company started owning vessels. (Under the guise of the North British Steam Packet Co. - the right of the rail companies to own ships was not recognised until an Act of Parliament in 1890.) The railway companies found that they had more control if they cut out the middle man and designed, built and operated for their own account. There was also a need to replace tonnage sold to the belligerents in the American Civil War. (Some private owners had taken a quick profit from these sales with scant regard to providing an estuary service.) As a result, in the years thereafter, the ownership of the fleets followed the fortunes of the rail companies and the dictates of national transport policies far removed from the shores of the Clyde. The Caledonian Railway (owner the Caledonian Steam Packet Co.) together with the Glasgow and South Western, became part of the London Midland and Southern Railway in 1923. At the same time the North British became part of the London North Eastern Railway. They were all incorporated into British Rail in the nationalisation of the railway industry in 1948 and the familiar company names disappeared. In 1969 the Caledonian Steam Packet was moved from railway control into the Scottish Transport Group alongside MacBrayne's Western Isles services. The Scottish Transport Group was itself re-shaped in 1973 and the result was today's largest operator of sea services in the Clyde, Caledonian MacBrayne.

To the Glaswegian an excursion on the river has to be savoured on a steamship, and a paddler for preference, if it is to have any flavour of authenticity; happily the continued existence of *ps Waverley* still allows this indulgence. Given the technology of the mid-nineteenth century it is not surprising that the paddler dominated at that time but why did the paddle continue to be used for propulsion until the 1950s and become part of the enduring legend?

Many of the Clyde's piers and jetties were at the landward end of the estuary's long fjord-like sea lochs and were in shallow water with difficult approaches due to shoals. While the paddle had progressively lost out to the propeller in the second half of the 1800s the paddler was a more shallow drafted vessel than the screw driven ship and was thus suited to the requirements of the upper reaches of the Clyde. Paddlers were also more manoeuvrable (turning could be facilitated by feathering or reversing one of the paddles) than a single screw ship. The railway companies, experts as they were in steam propulsion, brought the Clyde steamer to a new peak of efficiency. The steam turbine made its appearance in 1901, when the world's first commercial turbine driven passenger ship, *King Edward*, was built by

Denny of Dumbarton. But for all their efficiency these deep drafted ships could not be used throughout the Firth. So the paddler and the turbine co-existed, each plying its own trade, until they were both ousted by the marine diesel engine after World War II.

A trip down the river and into its estuary lives on in the Glasgow folk memory as one of innocent enjoyment of fresh air and scenery. And so it was and still is for many. But there could be a darker side to it. Glasgow, in the last quarter of the nineteenth century, was a bustling turbulent industrial city and not all of its citizens were of a saintly disposition. Some sought relief from the harsh conditions of everyday life and work in the consumption of intoxicating beverages and there were those who were prepared to cater for their needs.

Through the 1860s and 1870s two entrepreneurs by the names of Dewar and Sharp ran sailings on Sundays for those whose desire for a refreshment was curtailed by the closure of licensed premises on the Sabbath. They took advantage of the 1853 Forbes-McKenzie legislation which allowed those for whom travelling on a Sunday was a necessity i.e. those that travelled in all good faith, to obtain refreshment at their destination. Those who went afloat on Sharp and Dewar's ships, as bona fide travellers (or "Boney Feedy" in the Glasgow patois), quickly became inebriated. They got "steamboats" - the phrase became part of the

Not surprisingly, *Caledonia* was a name that was popular over the years with Scottish shipowners. This could be excused if your company's title was the Caledonian Steam Packet Co., for whom this version was built by Denny in 1934. A career which took her all over the Clyde in war and peace ended with her being taken to the Thames as a floating pub in 1969.

Caledonia 1934/620

West of Scotland vernacular - much to the righteous disgust of their more genteel fellow citizens looking on from the river banks. It was bad enough to offer excursions on a Sunday but to turn them into drinking binges was intolerable.

If you were to embark on a crusade against the demon drink afloat then you could do no better than to name your crusader for a well-known knight in shining armour. The Clyde Steam Packet Company Ltd. was set up to run alcohol free ships on River excursions and they called their ship *Ivanhoe* to fight the good fight for them. She operated from the douce and sober town of Helensburgh to Arran and beyond. Folklore has it that some of her passengers resorted to the contents of hip flasks to keep out the cold and to compensate for the ship's lack of amenity. (For a time such receptacles were known around Clydeside as "Ivanhoes".) The knight fell from grace when he came under the ownership of the Caledonian Steam Packet Company who promptly installed bars in the saloons.

In the 1880s legislation was to make it illegal to sell alcohol on a vessel which returned to its home port on the day of its departure and Dewar and Sharp went out of business. However the bona fide traveller stayed on the statute books for over a century until Scotland adopted a more liberal and realistic approach to alcohol consumption.

The troubles did not end there, for pocket-picking was rife on the crowded ships. Some were well-known for their gambling schools and warnings against card sharps were frequently made for the protection of the innocent Glaswegian. It is difficult at this distance to see sailing down the water in the same light as cruising the Mississippi in a stern-wheeler with its complement of colourful cigar-smoking gamblers but apparently this was not far removed from the truth.

Whatever the temptations and perils, the steamers were constantly in use between the Wars as a means of commuting to the far reaches of the Firth for business and pleasure. They had been marketed as an extension of the railway lines and with the changes in social habits that came after the 1950s they began to be seen as an extension of the road network. The foot passenger gave way to the car passenger and the paddlers and turbines became diesel driven vehicle ferries. The traditional piers fell into disuse as the motor car and better roads made the outreaches of the Firth more accessible. The remaining piers were converted to take vehicle ramps that adjusted to the tide.

The first car ferries were side-loading modifications of the diesel versions of the conventional Clyde steamers. In 1966 the first roll-on-roll-off vehicle ferry was introduced by what was to become Western Ferries (Argyll) Ltd. on the route from Kintyre to Islay and this mode was rapidly adopted for the remaining sea routes in the Firth of Clyde. In its various forms this is the type of ship that today serves the Clyde's remaining major destinations of Arran, Bute, Cumbrae and Cowal. They sail under the flags of Caledonian MacBrayne and Western Ferries.

The Yoker yard of Napier Shanks and Bell had to move to Old Kilpatrick to make way for the construction of Rothesay Dock and traded there until 1930 when the recession killed it off. It produced many fine ships and not least of them was the 1892 *Mercury* for the Glasgow and South Western Railway.

Her war experiences in 1914-18 were remarkable as in separate incidents she had her stern and then her bows blown off by mines. She survived to return to Clyde duties. Coincidentally, her 1934 replacement and namesake was mined and sunk in 1940. Perhaps it was a mistake to take the winged messenger out of his natural element.

Mercury 1892/380

The majestic *rmps Columba* qualified to have the title "royal mail" before her designation "paddle ship" by virtue of having a Post Office and mail sorting room on board. She delivered the mail at her various calling points in Loch Fyne on the Glasgow to Ardrishaig run which she served for fifty-eight years. At Ardrishaig it was possible to travel the Crinan Canal in the *Linnet* and then make a connection with another steamer for Oban.

A product of Thomson's yard at Clydebank she was capable of 21 knots and could travel the ninety miles from Glasgow to Ardrishaig in under six hours. In the winter months when her large capacity of 2,000 passengers was not needed she was laid up in Bowling harbour.

Her fine lines are apparent in the picture of her in drydock. At just over 300 feet, her length was eleven times her beam. This narrow hull form goes some way to explaining the speed she attained which was not bettered until the arrival of the turbines some twenty years later. Apart from the technical advantages the result was an elegant shape.

Columba 1878/540

The Glasgow and Inveraray Steamboat Co.'s *Lord of the Isles* rivalled *Columba* for elegance, if not quite for speed and size, on her voyages to upper Loch Fyne. She was a product of the Meadowside yard of D. & W. Henderson who were still building sailing ships in the 1890s.

By 1924, the date of this picture, she was owned by Turbine Steamers Ltd. and was operating to Bute. The holiday-makers in the rowing boats, to a man (and to a woman) without any buoyancy aids, do not seem perturbed by the imminence of the wake of such a large ship. The two on the left, for example, are completely engrossed in their transaction.

Lord of the Isles 1891/470

The North British Steam Packet Co. (in reality the North British Railway) ordered this, their second *Dandie Dinmont*, from Inglis' yard on the Kelvin. She connected their train services on the North bank of the River at Craigendoran to the Dunoon area. A typical turn of the century North British paddler, she still has her open bridge aft of her funnel. It would not only have been a wet and windy position for the helmsman, but on this evidence a sooty one as well.

In 1866 North British had taken delivery of an earlier *Dandie Dinmont* from Inglis thus beginning an association that lasted for eighty years. The Railway company favoured the titles of, or characters from, the novels of Sir Walter Scott when naming their ships.

Dandie Dinmont 1895/220

The Caledonian Steam Packet Co.'s *Duchess of Rothesay* was a product of Thomson's Clydebank yard in 1895 and ran on the Ardrossan to Arran route. She appears to be travelling at her reputed seventeen knots and the blast of steam issuing from her whistle is no doubt to warn the humble seven knot puffer of her approach.

She opened what was then Glasgow's latest port extension, Rothesay Dock, in 1907 by steaming into the new basin and breaking a ribbon stretched across the entrance. On board, was the Duke of Rothesay himself, otherwise the Prince of Wales and future King George V.

Duchess of Rothesay 1895/390

The paddle box of the North British Railway's *Talisman* is not particularly ornate, but does carry, appropriately enough, the figure of a twelfth century knight wreathed in thistles. Yet the same company (or rather its successor) when writing the specification for the *Jeannie Deans* called for "The paddle box carving... to be highly artistic in character."

Until the 1860s paddles usually had eight fixed wooden blades. A technological breakthrough came in 1864 when feathering steel blades were fitted to the *Iona*. The feathering blade was more efficient in driving the ship as the optimum aspect of the blade was presented to the water at the correct moment.

Talisman 1896/290

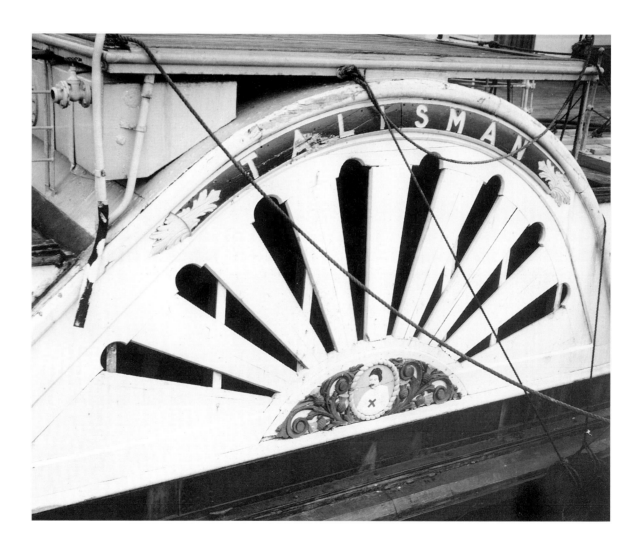

Two of the *Waverley* - although the Clyde has actually seen four since the 1820s. The single stack of the 1899 ship is in the red, white and black funnel colours of the North British Railway. She was bombed and sunk at Dunkirk in World War II.

The twin-funnelled 1947 version, like her predecessor a product of Inglis' Pointhouse yard, is the last of the Clyde's steam paddlers to survive. The Heritage Lottery Fund recently granted over £2 million for essential restoration to allow her to continue with her coastal excursions work. The lums are red, white and black again.

Waverley 1899/450 & 1947/690

The ships on these two pages are certainly not ferries in the accepted sense. Neither are they what the Glaswegian would regard as "doon the watter" boats. Clyde-built, they both survive to this day. They were strictly excursion ships but there is no argument that they carried folk across stretches of water that the Glaswegian regards as the "property" of his city. Certainly no one else dare lay claim to them.

This elegant little ship, soon to be a centenarian, still carries tourists on the waters of Loch Katrine in the Trossachs. Another of those re-assembly projects that some of the Clyde yards, which made their names in the construction of small specialist ships, always seemed to be producing. *Sir Walter Scott* came from Denny of Dumbarton.

Sir Walter Scott 1900/115

Today the *Maid of the Loch* is forlornly laid up at Balloch but, as an example of the last generation of inland paddle ships, she is a candidate for restoration to allow her to sail on Loch Lomond again. She was built at Inglis' yard at the mouth of the Kelvin before being taken to Balloch in sections. There she was assembled and launched. The popularity of cruising on the Loch has waxed and waned over the years and the *Maid* has changed owners several times. Perhaps local enthusiasm can revive her fortunes.

Maid of the Loch 1953/560

All three ships here were called *Glen Sannox*. (Two glens carry burns into Sannox Bay in the North-west corner of Arran.) They illustrate the progression from paddle ship to motor ship in over sixty years of the Clyde's "steamer" services.

The paddler, a product of Thomson at Clydebank, was capable of 20 knots and in conjunction with a Glasgow and South Western train it was possible at the turn of the century to get from Glasgow to Brodick in an hour and a half.

The second *Sannox*, a turbine steamer from Denny, was built for the London, Midland and Scottish Railway after the 1923 railway re-organisation and was also used on the Arran route.

The first two were much the same in overall dimensions and both could carry about 1,700 passengers. The third was larger in beam and while she was licensed for only 1,100 passengers she was able to answer the mid-1950s demand for vehicular traffic and take up to fifty cars.

Glen Sannox 1892/610, 1925/690, 1957/1,100

Juno and *Jupiter* always seemed to be paired when their owners were deciding on names for their newbuildings. Whether it was Reid and McKellar in the 1850s, Glasgow and South Western in the 1890s, London, Midland and Scottish in 1937 or latterly Caledonian MacBrayne, the two were never more than a year or so apart. What is more if they were not actually sister ships they were always very similar in size and characteristics.

Clearly a car ferry and equally clearly destined to run on one particular route, what is not obvious about this 1974 *Juno* is that she has no propellers but is driven and steered by her German designed Voith-Schneider units. In simple terms these are rather like paddles turned through 90 degrees - so really not much has changed in the field of marine engineering!

Juno 1974/850

Ever adventurous technically, Denny developed a version of the hovercraft. Their experimental *D2* is seen here on trials in May 1963. They never went into production with the concept and the money speculated on the experiment contributed to the decision to put the yard into liquidation in September of that same year. It was left to others to exploit the development of the hovercraft commercially.

The Clyde passenger trade flirted briefly with the hovercraft when in 1965 Clyde Hover Ferries Ltd. began a service using two Westland types on routes which took in the North and South banks, Dunoon, Rothesay and Tarbert. There were a variety of operational problems and the service did not re-start in 1966.

D2 1963

This is what "doon the watter" at the Glasgow Fair Holiday often meant - crowded decks under leaden grey skies. The date is 1921. *The Isle of Skye* had originally been the *Madge Wildfire*. From 1918 to 1927 she operated on Glasgow to Rothesay and Millport routes under the Williamson-Buchanan flag.

The Isle of Skye 1886/210

Across the Watter

While the river was a unifying force for the Clydesider it also divided him into Northsider and Southsider. Both banks were places of business and employment and that meant the river was for ever being crossed by those who lived and worked alongside it. At one time it could have been, and no doubt was, waded.

Adventurous Glaswegians can still try this, if they ignore the convenience of the Victoria Bridge, at low water spring tides at the East end of Carlton Place. It was from this spot that the Clyde Navigation Trust in 1884 began its zig-zag ferry service from North to South banks as far as Whiteinch and back. These ferries carried millions of Glasgow folk about their lawful businesses for nearly twenty years. (The little steam ships, which were romantically called Clutha after the ancient Roman name for the Clyde, were quite unromantically distinguished from each other by using numbers.) They were withdrawn in 1903 having lost too many customers to the Subway, which opened in 1896, and that other Glasgow institution of saintly memory, the Corporation's electric tramways, "the caurs" which came on the scene in 1901. The name lives on. The licensed premises, established in 1814, at the river end of Stockwell Street is the Clutha Vaults.

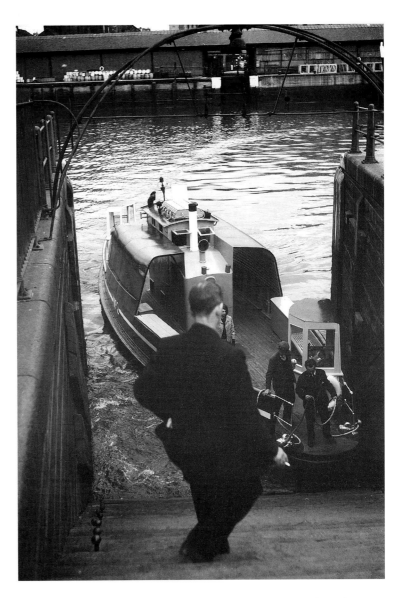

There was no charge on the cross-river ferries within the City boundary. They were, not unnaturally, a popular form of transport for the Glaswegian. Negotiating the steep and wet steps could require a certain amount of skill depending on how full the River - and the would-be passenger was. *No. 2*, seen here, was the first diesel powered ferry and operated between the north bank at Clyde Street and the Kingston Dock. This service closed at the end of 1966.

Clyde River Ferry No. 2 1934

Prior to the Clutha service there had not been new road bridges over the Clyde west of the Glasgow Bridge since 1835. The completion of the King George V Bridge in 1927 scarcely improved this situation as it was only a matter of a few hundred yards nearer the sea. The Subway and the Finnieston Tunnel (this also opened in 1896) were essentially City centre facilities and yet the river, its towns and its industries stretched to Dumbarton on the north side and to Greenock on the south with only these two physical crossings

The Clyde Navigation Trust was charged with providing services on and adjacent to the River. As its powers were extended by various Acts of Parliament, specifically that of 1840, it took over the established cross-river ferries, some of which had their origins in rowing boat services of unknown antiquity. There was certainly a ferry for horse and carriage traffic at Renfrew in the 18th century.

The Clutha service was not the Trust's first venture into the ferry business. It had taken over the Govan Ferry in 1857 and had introduced a steam ferry between the north bank and the Kingston Dock area in 1865. In 1911 it assumed control of the Burgh of Renfrew's vehicle ferry service to Yoker on the north bank. This had originally been established as a chain-hauled steam-powered service in 1868. It was possible for the Clydesider to cross the river at up to eight different locations until after World War II.

A particular feature of the Glasgow cross-river routes was the elevating vehicular ferry. Somewhat ungainly in

The Meadowside ferry, *Ferry No. 4*, is approaching the south bank at Fairfield's yard. She does not look overcrowded here and indeed the service, together with the nearby Govan ferry, ceased in November 1965 no doubt due to the much reduced level of activity in that stretch of the River. Seven nearby shipyards had closed in 1963-64.

Clyde River Ferry No. 4 1928

appearance but highly practical in operation, these craft could load cars and lorries at any state of the tide by raising and lowering the platform unto which vehicles could drive from the riverside roads. The first Vehicular Ferry was introduced to link Finnieston and Plantation Quays in 1890. At the peak of their operations there were four vehicle ferries for three crossing points, at Govan, Finnieston and Whiteinch.

This drive-on facility turned *Vehicular Ferry No. 4* into a highly effective fire fighting ship in 1940. The cruiser HMS *Sussex* was bombed at Yorkhill and her fuel oil ignited. The fire was spreading to her magazines and had these exploded a wide area would have been devastated. *No. 4* was manoeuvred alongside and used as a fire-fighting platform. The blaze was controlled and the danger to the nearby Yorkhill Hospital was averted.

The building and maintenance of the ships for these utilities was of course a source of economic benefit to Clydeside's industries. The smaller yards in particular produced a range of vessels to suit the needs of the travelling public. The downside was that as cross-river transport facilities changed the yards suffered when the ferries were withdrawn. But while the ship remained as the logical and cost effective manner in which to go "across the watter", Fleming and Ferguson of Paisley, Seath and Company of Rutherglen, Ferguson of Port Glasgow and their ilk all played their part in providing the means.

The first tunnel under the River, at Finnieston, had separate underpasses for pedestrian and horse-drawn traffic. Such was the volume of traffic in that part of the city that it co-existed with the nearby ferry for many years even after the horse and cart disappeared from the streets. The second, at Whiteinch, referred to today as the Clyde Tunnel, was a twin bore dual carriageway linked to Clydeside's urban motorway network. Its southern access was built near the site of the defunct shipyard of Alexander Stephen and its opening brought about the closure of the Whiteinch ferry service in December 1963.

If the 1960s was the period of the closure of the Clydeside shipyards it was also the decade of the withdrawal of the ferry services. The two were linked of course. Fewer people worked on the actual banks of the river and when they did travel they wanted go beyond the immediate confines of the waterside and they crossed on four wheels. Two new bridges were to administer the "coup de grace". In January 1967 the Clyde Street ferry closed when construction work started on the Kingston Bridge. It had been one of the last of the services at the city end of the river; most of the others having gone in 1965/66. (Renovation work on the Subway gave a temporary lifeline to the Kelvinhaugh ferry but it was withdrawn too on the re-opening of the Subway in 1980.) The high level box girder toll-bridge at Erskine opened in 1971, and another ferry disappeared. The Renfrew ferry struggled on into the 1980s, its operating deficit subvented by an understanding local authority who kept open an ambulance link on otherwise pedestrian only vessels.

The motor car, the subway, the electrified trains, the buses, the tunnels and the bridges, all manifestations of progress and the central planning of transport, had combined to undermine another piece of the Clyde's marine heritage.

Vehicle Ferry No. 4 (as a breed they were always given this full title, with the number as the only variation) was propelled by diesel electric machinery which also lowered and raised the platform to suit the state of the tide on the River. She is about to dock on the south side at Harland and Wolff's yard shortly before it closed in 1963. The entrance to A. & J. Inglis' yard at the mouth of the Kelvin can be seen at the right of the picture.

Vehicle Ferry No. 4 1938

The Empire Exhibition at Bellahouston Park in 1938 created enormous interest in the Glasgow area and beyond. The Caledonian Steam Packet Co. cashed in by offering River cruises from the City centre at Bridge Wharf to the Exhibition. Two motor ferries were commissioned from Denny at Dumbarton for the purpose. *Ashton* and *Leven* carried 112 passengers and the popular service was carried on until the start of World War II.

Leven 1938

A chain-hauled and steam-driven ferry had operated from Renfrew to Yoker from 1868 under the auspices of the local Renfrew Town Council. (The origins of a ferry service at this point go back to at least the sixteenth century.) In 1911 the service was taken over by the Clyde Navigation Trust. This is the "new" *Renfrew Ferry* of 1936 - but still chain hauled and steam propelled. It was not until 1952 that a diesel-electric vessel appeared on the route. This was a busy and popular ferry with the shipyard workers on the north bank and those bound for Hillington on the south.

Renfrew Ferry 1936

The first Cluthas were constructed at Seath's yard at Rutherglen. Later versions came from Murray Bros at Dumbarton and Russell and Co. of Port Glasgow and these like *Clutha No. 5*, seen here with Partick Pier in the background, were generally longer and carried over three hundred people.

The Clyde Navigation Trust bought a dozen of these craft between 1884 and 1891 and they sailed to and fro across the River from north to south and from the Broomielaw to Whiteinch and back. The service began at 5 a.m. to allow workers to get to the yards for the morning shift. (Since the service was withdrawn in 1903, when Dan McDonald was four years old, these pictures could not have been taken by him. Nevertheless the negative is in his Collection and, as such, qualifies for insertion here.)

Clutha No. 5 1887

The reader might well wonder how the Forth Railway Bridge gets into a selection of photographs dedicated to the Clyde. The inclusion of Scotland's hero king is not an overt act of nationalism. The fact that the *Robert the Bruce* was a diesel-electric paddler and the first all-welded ship in Scotland would be better reason. (The complementary vessel of this two ship service was *Sir William Wallace*.) The link with the Clyde is that she was built and owned by Denny of Dumbarton. Why were the Edinburgh shipowners prepared to let a Glaswegian onto their river?

Robert the Bruce 1934

The Watter, Deep and Clean

The Clyde Navigation Trust's Hopper No. 2 *passes Dumbarton Rock on her way down-river to dump dredged spoil at Garroch Head.*
Hopper No. 2 1903/830

Port Glasgow was just that - the port of Glasgow - for it was as far up the shallow, shoaled River Clyde as the quite modestly drafted ships of the mid-nineteenth century could navigate.

To get his goods to the City, the Glasgow merchant had depended on horse-drawn barges up to 1812 or the so-called "luggage boats" after steam propulsion arrived. These barges often made their way to the City by the Forth and Clyde Canal the entrance of which was at Bowling. In the 1840s he could depend on the Glasgow to Greenock railway. He could not bring sea-going ships upstream to the town's wharves; not unless they were lightened at the Tail of the Bank. Glasgow was very much a subsidiary port to Greenock, Newark and Dumbarton; that is until a conscious effort was made to deepen the river.

In the late 1700s and early 1800s systems of dykes had been built in the river to encourage the natural flow of water to sweep a deeper channel, but little more than four feet of water could be expected at low tide even when *Comet* made her epoch making first voyage in 1812. The old and proven method of dragging ploughs across the river bed by means of capstans fixed on the banks had its obvious limitations and it was not really until 1824, when a steam dredger appeared, that the deepening and straightening of the Clyde by effective mechanical means began. The removal of silt and sandbanks often revealed rock outcrops on the river bed and these had to be laboriously blasted and

excavated so it was as late as 1870 before a depth of twenty feet at low water could be guaranteed over the length of the main channel. With a tidal range of the order of three metres, perhaps nearly four metres at spring tides, an operating depth of thirty feet or more could be achieved.

This was gradually improved upon until the depth of thirty-eight feet, required by the ocean-going liners that the

River was producing, could be relied on. Even then there were occasional accidents. Probably the best known was when the *Queen Mary*, on her maiden passage down the river grounded at the Dalmuir bend; tugs and the tide brought her off without damage.

Constant dredging to maintain these channel depths was required and the Clyde Navigation Trust bought a dredger from the Renfrew yard of Wm. Simons and Co. in 1862 and thus began a relationship that was to last almost a century. It was the first dredger that the Trust ordered for its own account and it was the first dredger that Simons built.

At first the spoil from dredging was dumped at various carefully chosen locations along the riverside and when this became impracticable the deep fjord-like Loch Long was chosen as a repository for the unwanted silt and rock. (It was recounted in 1840 that 150,000 cubic yards of silt from the river had been deposited and spread on the Whiteinch farm! Crop yields were reported to be higher as a consequence.) For the transport of the spoil the Clyde Navigation Trust built and operated a fleet of hoppers to work in conjunction with the dredgers. (With a typical institutional lack of imagination they were given numbers, up to *No. 28.*) However, as a result of complaints from residents in the Loch Long area (there were NIMBYs even in those days) the dump site was changed to Garroch Head off the south end of Bute.

The Clyde Trust collected harbour dues from ships using the port according to their registered tonnage. Hence the deepening and widening of the river paid handsome rewards commercially as larger ships traded to the port and the yards launched bigger vessels. In more recent times the pendulum has swung the other way. As commercial activity declined the dredging of the upper reaches of the harbour became unviable financially. In recent times a decision not to dredge the River above Yarrow's yard at Scotstoun was reversed after the local authority agreed to make a contribution to the costs. Otherwise there could have been a restriction on the activity of Kvaerner's yard at Govan and the possibility of a flooded Buchanan Street when the storm drains silted up.

Glasgow's burgeoning nineteenth century industrial prosperity was sustained by a population explosion. A bi-product of this was that huge quantities of untreated sewage poured into the Clyde. By all accounts the stench in the upper reaches could be intolerable and this may have contributed to the relative unpopularity of the "all the way" steamer sailings from the Broomielaw to the towns and resorts in the lower reaches of the estuary. (By taking the train to Gourock before catching the steamer the nose would have been less offended.) On the other hand those increased crop yields at the Whiteinch Farm are now explained.

The risk to public health may not have been as well understood as it is today and the offence to the senses may have been the motivation, but the City of Glasgow eventually acted to set up works for the treatment of sewage. Three plants were built, between 1894 and 1910, at Dalmarnock, Dalmuir and Shieldhall, as a result of which the River in the City became a less noisome place, public health was much improved and sailing from Bridge Wharf could again be described as a pleasure cruise.

However, sewage treatment plants also have their bi-products. Their large quantities of not unhealthy, but unattractive sludge, had to be spirited away from the public gaze somehow. The solution was found in the purchase and conversion of an oil tanker to carry the treated sewage down to the sea for dumping. (The Loch Long lesson having been learned the effluent went straight to Garroch Head to join the other detritus of the River.) The Clydesiders became fond of their "sludge boats" (they were given local names, the first being the *Dalmuir*) and they became popular for free day-trips down the river for groups of Senior Citizens.

The sludge boats are due to disappear in 1998 as EEC regulations come into force which will outlaw this type of dumping. It is technically feasible to pelletise the sludge in a form which will make it suitable for combustion in the furnaces of power stations. This is likely to happen and it is consistent with the modern philosophy of environmental sensitivity, but the river will become an emptier place in more ways than one.

Forty five years separate these two versions of the *Dalmarnock*. Both were the Clyde Trust's sludge boats, named after one of the sewage treatment plants built at the turn of the century. Both were designed to take the treated effluent to Garroch Head for dumping and their appearances reflect forty-five years of changes in naval architecture. The older steamer is returning light ship while the newer motor ship is clearly heavily laden and outward bound to relieve herself of her burden.

Dalmarnock 1925/1370 & 1970/840

While anchored in the middle of the busy River near Finnieston a self-discharging hopper *(No. 7)* has silt transferred to her from a dredger alongside. This process went on continuously to maintain the depth of the Clyde in the upper reaches.

Hopper No. 7 1911/830

Lobnitz produced the bucket dredger, *Rosslyn*, seen here working with her attendant hopper, *No. 5*, at the Broomielaw. The huge superstructure and driving wheels for the buckets give her a distinctive profile.

Rosslyn 1912/900

The digger barge, *Sir William H. Raeburn*, was ordered from Ferguson Bros by the Clyde Lighthouse Trust, (this body was assumed into the Clyde Port Authority) whose chairman Raeburn had been. She is working in the city, by the Suspension Bridge. In 1949 there was still enough River traffic to justify the operation. The buildings in the background are still there today but the sheds have gone; replaced by a landscaped walkway.

Sir William H. Raeburn 1928/250

No. 27, (opposite page, bottom) the Clyde Navigation Trust's second diesel hopper, is of the same basic design as her steam predecessors but the self-discharge mechanism is hydraulically controlled. She was one of the last of the Simons and Lobnitz designed ships. No. 26 (opposite page, top), her immediate predecessor by eight years, was the last of the steamer hoppers but in appearance is scarcely distinguishable from No. 3 (above) which dates from 1926.

No. 3 1926/670
No. 26 1954/940
No. 27 1962/980

"Gallus", is the only adjective that can be applied here. For those not familiar with the West of Scotland patois, the meaning of the word is perfectly conveyed by this gentleman's demeanour. With bunnet angled, the fag couched in the best Noel Coward fashion and the telegraph at "Full Ahead" he may be the steersman of a humble hopper, but he would not give way to the *Queen Mary*.

Pulling and Pushing

The tight tow line is graphic illustration of the "art" of towage. The tug's rope is spliced to a steel wire which is passed through the warship's fairlead and secured to the bitts on her foredeck. She is flying two balls from her mast halyard to indicate that she is not under her own command but under the control of the tug.

There must have been a towage activity on the Clyde from the earliest days of steam propulsion. Henry Bell's *Comet* is known for its passenger carrying activities but the sequence of wooden-hulled steamers that followed her from the builders' yards, the early luggage boats, were known to have pulled barges of merchandise from Greenock and Port Glasgow up river to the City. Certainly by 1818, six years after the appearance of *Comet*, a paddle steamer named *Samson* was being referred to as a 'tug-boat'. She was originally constructed for the more serious purpose of assisting sailing vessels to get to their destinations against adverse winds and tides.

The suffix came to be dropped and the generic name of 'Tug' was applied to the small powerful vessel designed to aid other ships berth and unberth. Indeed in 1817 a vessel was built in Dumbarton for the purpose of towing ships from Leith to Grangemouth. She was named simply, *Tug*, which described her function admirably.

By its very nature the shallow and winding Clyde was a tugowner's heaven. Even when it ceased to be shallow (relatively), it still offered a narrow channel, three hundred feet across, at best. The high volume of traffic that was to characterise the Clyde and the confines in which it had to travel called for the closest control of all types of ships. The steamer or motor ship was no exception to this requirement for they had least control of their own movements when they were operating at low speed and subject to the forces of wind and tide. As the Clyde expanded as a commercial port five major docks were cut into her banks all with relatively narrow entrances and most with several tongues with discharging berths on both sides. In all this close quarter manoeuvring the deep sea ship needed the presence of a pilot and the skills of well controlled tugs.

In the 1850s there were seven towage companies on the River and the Estuary employing about fifty tugs. They were all steam driven paddle-ships and with one exception their hulls were constructed in wood. Over the next ten years iron replaced wood in newbuildings. Steam, in its various developments and improvements in power and fuel efficiency, held sway as the driving force for another hundred years before giving way to diesel. Screw propelled tugs appeared in the 1880s but the last paddle tug was not taken out of service until 1948, at the age of fifty.

As the type of ship to be handled grew larger, tugs had to become more powerful to exert the necessary correcting forces upon them. An engine output of fifty to one hundred horsepower had served well enough up to 1850, but after that engine sizes rose steadily until two thousand five hundred horsepower became the norm in the 1970s. The tug fleet size had followed the general shipping trend of "fewer but larger" and the tugs of the 1970s were designed to service the large tankers using the oil terminal at Finnart

in Loch Long which had become operational during World War II. Probably the largest commercial ship to use the Clyde was a 286,000 ton deadweight tanker that was berthed there with the assistance of six tugs.

Over the years by a process of acquisition and as a consequence of some commercial failures the number of towage companies shrank to two. Both had grown from the same root; the Clyde Shipping Co. Ltd., a joint stock company established in 1815. After its sale in 1856 by the group of merchants who founded it, Clyde Shipping was broken up. The name was retained by one new grouping of four shareholders but some of the assets went to the company's then manager whose company eventually evolved into Steele and Bennie and Co. Ltd. Competition between Steele and Bennie and Clyde Shipping for the River's towage business was fierce and bitter with the parties resorting to law on more than one occasion. Some remnants of this rivalry were still to be seen a century later, but in 1962 the two companies entered into a consortium agreement to co-operate in servicing the River, and much time, effort and operating costs were saved by this sensible arrangement.

Steele and Bennie was acquired from its family interests in 1971 by Cory Ship Towage, a Liverpool based subsidiary of the then Ocean Transport and Trading Company. By 1995 the Clyde's towage fleet had been reduced to four tugs as a consequence of the downturn in shipping activity and Clyde Shipping sold out to Cory.

Some of those vessels that still use the River still need to be pushed onto their berths or pulled from them. For as long as ships come to the Clyde this is likely to be the case. The tradition and service initiated in 1815 still continues.

With a tightening line to an unseen ship, *pt Samson* backs into mid-river. The paddlers were very manoeuvrable, more so than their single screw driven sisters, and were often used as the stern tug "on the drag". But they could not compete for pulling power and gradually they were replaced. *Samson* served for another five years after the date of this picture before going to the breakers in 1933.

Samson 1896/150

For a large part of her career *Flying Fish* was stationed at what is now Cobh in the south of Ireland. (After 1856 Clyde Shipping Co. adopted the pre-fix "Flying" when naming its tugs.) From there, she went out into the Western Approaches and the Bristol Channel to seek for sailing ships which required to be towed to UK ports against adverse winds. It was from Cobh in 1915 that she went to the aid of the stricken *Lusitania*. She was first on the scene and picked up two hundred and forty survivors.

Flying Fish 1886/140

During World War II the Admiralty built a series of harbour tugs based on a Steele and Bennie design. Many of these were later sold to commercial towage companies. Clyde Shipping Co. bought several and gave them the names of fighter aircraft, like *Flying Hurricane*. In the interests of securing a good bargain Clyde Shipping swallowed its pride and bought a tug conceived by its oldest rival.

Flying Hurricane 1942/250

Steele and Bennie chose names with a martial ring to them for their tugs. Their other distinguishing feature was the black and white banded funnel. (Clyde Shipping's lums were all black.) *Battleaxe* is a good example of a between-the-wars steam tug and she is seen here towing a City liner on very short and steeply angled tow rope. This was an effective method of controlling ships in tight spaces like the Glasgow docks but it left very little room for error. It is not difficult to imagine how easily the tug could be run down by the larger ship.

Battleaxe 1928/230

Towing other ships is not without its dangers. Steele and Bennie's *Forager* was capsized by the tow rope from the New Zealand Shipping Co.'s *Hororta*, which caught her funnel. When 14,000 grt meets 200 it is an unequal contest. Steele and Bennie tugs often featured large and well-raked lums. They may have been designed with the aesthetics of the vessel in mind but the cynical claimed that it made their tugs look more powerful than they really were.

Even before the days when the interaction between hulls of ships in close proximity was fully understood there were remarkably few instances of accidental contact between tugs and the ships they were assisting. *Forager* was raised, repaired at Stephens and sold to Italy.

Forager 1945/240

Steele and Bennie's *Chieftain* still has the sharp stem of the nineteenth century tugs but she carries a rope fender for pushing duties. Later tugs were to have their stems modified with large rubberised fenders built-in to increase the effective pushing area. She carries a curious mixture of seaman-like worked rope fenders and the functional but landlubberly old tyres along her rubbing strip.

Chieftain 1930/200

Three Clyde Shipping tugs, led by the *Flying Kite*, are about to leave Queen's Dock for duty in 1929. She was to be the River's only tug casualty of World War II. She struck a mine or sunken bomb at Dalmuir in 1941 and became a total loss. Regrettably, her master and four of her crew were killed.

Flying Kite 1929/240

Steele and Bennie's *Chieftain* with her sister, *Campaigner*, is backing the *Empire Halladale* out of dock while *Strongbow*, waits to take a rope to the ship's bow.

The crew of the *Cruiser* manhandle the twelve inch manila hawser towards the towing hook set aft of the wheelhouse casing. A three inch wire is already fixed onto the bitts of the ship which is to be plucked off her berth. Clyde tugs always sent up their own gear to a ship; that way the quality of the essential link was kept in the hands of the tugowner.

This shot of the after deck of the diesel tug *Brigadier* shows the typical towing arrangements of the time. The tow line is fixed on the towing hook which can rotate through an arc of about 180 degrees on its semi-circular track. It is draped over the tow bars which keep it clear of the engine room casing and the deck. A windlass is fixed aft to control the so called "gob rope" which served to keep the tow line in line with the fore and aft axis of the tug. This was to prevent the tug being pulled sideways by the weight of the vessel she was towing.

Brigadier 1961/220

Flying Scout was the first of the Clyde's diesel tugs to dispense with the traditional funnel by using simple uprights to evacuate the engine exhaust. The loss of the lum gave much improved visibility aft for the tug master. This was no small consideration since most of this tug's work was behind her.

Flying Scout 1970/230

While the hull shape of this *Fulmar* may be quite traditional the superstructure is dramatically unusual. The power is provided by twin Polar engines whose emissions are taken away by flues in the tall structure that carries the firefighting monitors. The result is a functional and visually pleasing profile.

The top monitor is twenty-one metres above the waterline and it was able, if necessary, to spray fire-quenching foam on the decks of the large tankers that visited the Finnart Oil Terminal in Loch Long. Finnart was connected with the refinery at Grangemouth by a cross-country pipeline. After oil from the Forties Field started to come directly ashore from the North Sea to the Forth the importance of Finnart was greatly diminished.

Flying Fulmar 1974/300

Hugh Cameron was master in the Clyde Shipping tug fleet for many years. A slightly posed shot on the *Flying Fulmar* shows this worthy in 1949, hand on the engine room telegraph, dressed in a formality (double-breasted suit, collar, tie and cap) that the modern skipper would eschew.

Small was Equally Beautiful

Gem Line's *Jacinth*, owned by the long established Glasgow shipping family of Wm. Robertson steams up-river past Langbank. A typical late nineteenth century steamer built for the middle trades by a typical medium sized Clyde-based company. The theme for naming the fleet was precious or semi-precious stones.

Jacinth 1888/500

The fame of the Clyde did not rest only its large ships. Warships, huge luxury liners, and world-ranging shipping companies were all very well but many lines and ships operated much closer to home and with more modest means. In their way they were just as profitable, well-managed and technically sound concerns as their more glamorous fellow Clydesiders. They, too, kept the yards busy and the ancillary industries employed.

The West of Scotland needed connections with Ireland, North and South, England and continental Europe, all of whom wanted its coal and its industrial products. The Home and Middle Trades, as they were known, were busy with the ships of Glasgow interests.

Daily services between the Clyde and Northern Ireland were maintained and thrice weekly sailings for passengers and goods for Cork and Waterford were on offer for nigh on a hundred years until the 1960s. These were the "liner" services. This simply meant that the ships sailed on a pre-determined schedule to the same destinations. They were not to be confused with, for example, the Cunard type of liner. Having a regular timetable meant that they were not "tramps".

In the language of the marine world the word, "tramp", is not the derogatory description applied on land to the vagrant. Many fine vessels were tramps and they were operated by companies who kept the highest standards. The liner owner said, "Here we are going from A to B twice per week. Our rates are competitive so come along and fill up our ship". The skills required to be a successful tramp owner were quite different. The tramp owner had to play a game of three dimensional chess, frequently moving his pieces about the board. He was constantly in the market place moving his ships around to keep them loaded as much as possible to maximise his earnings. He loaded his ship for a port and he knew approximately, given reasonable weather conditions, when it would be discharged and available again. Could he load again at that port or should he make a lightship passage to pick up a lucrative cargo that he was committed to some days later at another port? Sailing empty was unprofitable but if he tried to fit in another cargo from his discharging port would he be late for his commitment? And so it went on. Much more fun really.

In design terms the ships of the liner companies came to be quite different from those of the tramps. The liners developed as passenger carriers with holds for mixed freight rather than for bulk cargoes such as coal or grain. The tramps on the other hand carried bulk or general cargoes -

their hazardous schedule, or lack of any schedule, made them unattractive to passengers desiring to reach a destination by a given date.

Both types were to lose out to the same general changes in the nature and methods of transport that arrived with the 1960s.

In 1965 the Boeing 707, that icon of inexpensive mass air travel, came into operation.

People were wooed away by the airlines and chose to fly to Belfast and Amsterdam rather than go by ship. Passenger planes had always carried some freight in their holds, but they were overtaken in tonnage carried by the mid-1960s by the specialised freight only aircraft. Ten years later Heathrow Airport was considered to be the UK's biggest port.

Containerisation, road haulage and the roll-on-roll-off ship, developed in America in the 1950s, soon captured the rest of the general cargo market. Together they offered a door-to-door service at attractive cost and could do so because of reduced handling costs and the shorter time spent by the ship in port.

Some bulk cargoes could be containerised to an extent, coal was an example, but the difference in the post war period was that the size of a ship was driven by the economics of scale. To succeed it had to become an 80,000 tonner and not an 8,000 tonner. Few of the small to medium sized Clydeside firms could command the markets to fill such ships or had the financial strength to invest in them. So they withdrew from the battle.

Today there is a single, overnight, freight only, roll-on-roll-off ship running from Ardrossan to Belfast.

For around a hundred years from 1856 onwards Clyde Shipping Co. ran a coastal liner service from the Clyde to Ireland, the Bristol Channel and the Thames. They named their ships after lighthouses and *Eddystone* is a fair example of their 1920s design. She is also seen here (below) in her wartime grey with a gun mounted aft and with quick release life rafts installed. These relatively small ships were requisitioned in World War II and sent out in Atlantic convoys to act as Rescue Ships. Their duty, from a station at the rear of the convoy, was to rescue from the water the crews of vessels torpedoed by the enemy. Seven of Clyde's ships were employed on such duties and two were lost carrying them out.

Eddystone 1927/1500

A few yards from her owner's office in the heart of Glasgow, *St Enoch* sits on the bottom discharging sand. She has had to lower her lum to get under the City bridges. On the next berth lies an unknown puffer and the bow of the Royal Naval Volunteer Reserve's *sv Carrick* can be seen ahead of her. The sandy bottom of the River protrudes into the bottom of the picture showing the shallow nature of the undredged River in the upper reaches.

St Enoch 1918/360

J. & A. Gardner is one of the few surviving Glasgow based coasting companies and for many years it had its office in the heart of the City at Clyde Street. Its directors named their ships after the saints of the old Celtic Church. Though it traded to the West Highlands, often with stone from the company's own quarry at Bonawe in Loch Etive, its ships were too grand to be classed with the puffers. *St Aidan* though, came from the pufferman's yard - Scotts of Bowling.

St Aidan 1920/360

The *Hebrides* was built at the Ailsa Shipyard at Troon to run with passengers and general cargo from the Clyde to the Western Highlands. She had belonged to a company called McCallum Orme which was absorbed into David MacBrayne. Most notably she played a part in the evacuation of St. Kilda in 1930.

Hebrides 1898/590

Wm. Robertson's *Onyx* was built at Bowling and stayed in their fleet until 1937.
She survived under other owners until she was broken up in 1952. "Clydebuilt"
really did mean durability!

Onyx 1910/590

The history of Coast Lines is a complex one and the company only came to be known as Coast Lines Ltd. when it went public in 1919. Burns and Laird Ltd. were well known for their overnight sailings between the West of Scotland and Northern Ireland. G. & J. Burns had started their Glasgow to Belfast run in 1849 and the Laird's Line had been in coastal services from at least 1835. In 1920, both were taken over by Coast Lines who amalgamated them to form Burns and Laird.

After 1929 all the ships were renamed and carried the prefix "Laird". *Lairdsgrove* had been acquired second-hand but the Inglis-built ship served them well - until 1948 when she was fifty years old. The *Lairdscastle* was typical of the company's combined passenger and cargo ships of the period between the Wars. It was mostly a case of people out and agricultural produce back.

The *Lairds Loch* had been built at the Ardrossan Dockyard in 1945 and was one of the last vessels to ply the Scotland to Ireland routes for Burns and Laird. She was sold in 1969 when the Glasgow to Belfast run was closed. (The Dublin service had ceased at the beginning of 1968.) Coast Lines itself was taken over by P. & O. in 1971.

Lairdsgrove 1898/1200
Lairdscastle 1924/1950
Lairds Loch 1945/1500

In the summer months *Loch Fyne* took excursionists round the Mull to Staffa and Iona under the MacBrayne flag. She was innovative as the first diesel-electric vessel to ply the West Coast. Her twin screws were driven by direct current generators which in turn derived their power from diesel engines. Economy rather than speed was the product of this propulsion system.

Loch Fyne 1931/750

The Clyde Puffer

A puffer on the Clyde. The *Pibroch* steams up the river of her birth.

Although it was born on a canal and it was for many years to be seen on Scotland's East coast as much as its West, the puffer seems destined to be known as the "Clyde Puffer".

The Forth and Clyde Canal was completed in 1792 and connected Grangemouth in the East with Bowling in the West. Goods traversed the Canal in small sailing ships or in horse-drawn barges. A brave attempt was made in 1803 to introduce steam propulsion to this conduit when the stern-paddle ship, *Charlotte Dundas*, successfully towed two laden barges from Castlecary to Port Dundas in Glasgow. She was not considered to be appropriate for the Canal and wind and horse power continued to provide the driving force for vessels for another fifty years.

While the canal men languished in their technical backwater great things were happening outside the confines of their waterway. The first iron hull in Scotland had been built in 1819 and since the demonstration of the possibilities that were promised by the *Comet*, the marine steam engine was an instrument of proven capabilities. In the 1840s it became accepted that the propeller was superior to the paddle for driving a hull through water and the iron hull gave the craft the rigidity that was needed for the long tailshaft that connected the engine to the propeller. In 1856 the management of the Forth and Clyde Canal brought all these elements together and installed a two cylinder steam engine and a propeller in an iron scow called *Thomas*. A year later a purpose-built canal ship, called appropriately

enough, *Glasgow*, was constructed at Swann's yard at Hamiltonhill on the Canal. They were the first of a breed to be known for ever after as "puffers".

They earned this soubriquet from the fact that their early steam engines exhausted their steam directly into the atmosphere with a loud puffing noise, not unlike that to be heard in the present day from vintage steam locomotives. They stopped puffing when condensers were fitted and the water was recycled back to the boiler. This improved their operating range and they gradually replaced the sailing

Hamilton and McPhail's *Glenrosa* is discharging coal at Lochboisdale, South Uist. She was a wartime VIC and the puffer owners bought her from the Admiralty and spent a tidy sum fitting her out to their standards. The bucket swinging at the end of the derrick was the standard measure for coal in the West Highlands. When a community's Coal Club ordered a winter's supply it organised the purchase of the coal and the payment of the freight. Locally it was responsible for supervising the fair distribution of the coal and collecting cash in proportion to the number of buckets each household had received.

Glenrosa 1944/99

gabbarts as the prime mover of cargoes of eighty to one hundred tons on the Forth and Clyde and on the East and West coasts of Scotland.

They were built well inland, on the Canal at Kirkintilloch. Two yards, J. & J. Hay Ltd. and P. McGregor and Company Ltd. became famous as builders of these supremely useful vessels. They were constructed to fit the Canal's locks and were therefore restricted to a length of sixty-six, a beam of eighteen and a draft of nine feet. This meant that they could also traverse the Crinan Canal, which could take ships of a length of eighty-eight feet, for quick access from the Clyde to the Western Islands. Some eighty-eight footers were built by Clyde yards, notably Scotts of Bowling, but the vast majority stuck to Forth and Clyde size limits.

This was the classic puffer that became the willing workhorse of the West Highlands. They would go anywhere and carry anything. They became famous for sailing up the beach in remote nooks and crannies and unloading their cargoes over the side after the tide had receded. The closure of the Forth for security reasons during the 1914-18 War dealt a death blow to the East coast trade and, in the popular imagination and in reality, they became wholly associated with the West coast and its Highlands and Islands.

They remained virtually unaltered in design and size until after World War II when the first diesel driven puffer, the *Glenshira*, was produced from Bowling in 1953. She was made to Crinan limits and could therefore carry more cargo than the sixty-six footers. This was an important economic consideration. Other diesels followed and after the Forth and Clyde was closed to traffic in 1962 further economic pressure and dissatisfaction with the Crinan, where water shortage was often a problem, caused the puffer owners to turn to a different design.

The major owners started building vessels of one hundred and ten feet in length, which could carry cargoes of two hundred and forty tons of coal. They had to make passages round the Mull of Kintyre but were capable of doing so with some ease and the economic advantage of the earnings from the larger cargo outweighed the cost of the longer sailing time.

They had to squeeze every efficiency that they could from their methods of operation for their market shrank in the 1960s. Improved and extended road networks made many of their traditional delivery points more accessible to the commercial vehicle. The introduction of the roll-on-roll-off ferry to West Highland sea routes further reinforced the attractions of road haulage. In particular the fierce price war that raged between two ferry companies on the profitable Islay route drove the puffers out of their most important single market.

The remaining puffer companies rationalised themselves into a single company in 1968 but in the face of competition from a nationally subsidised ferry company the puffers were losing money by the late 1970s. In 1979 they applied for and received a subsidy from Government to carry on with their "lifeline" services of bulk cargoes and for a few years all was well. The subsidy was withdrawn in 1988 and although the remaining puffers struggled on for another few years the curtain was brought down on a 130 year-old tradition of service in 1993.

Hay's *Gael* lies with a group of puffers in the upper River in 1922 at a time
when some of the traffic on the Clyde still depended on sail-power.
Gael 1897/85

Passing Hogarth's *Baron Haig* under tow in the River, *X* typifies the late nineteenth century canal boat design. She was built for the Leith, Hull and Hamburg Steam Packet Company Ltd. who used the letters of the alphabet to name their puffers. Despite the sophistication of a wheel, rather than a tiller, she leaves her helmsman completely exposed to the elements and he and the other two crewmen would have shared a fifteen foot space in the fo'c'sle for their accommodation. Her main purpose in life would have been to ship goods from the Forth to the Clyde and she would not have ventured outside the confines of either river.

X of Leith 1882/80

Northern Ireland, as well as Scotland, enjoyed a good reputation as a place to build puffers. *Faithful*, originally owned by Warnock Brothers of Paisley, was a product of the Larne Shipbuilding Co. She earned herself a certain notoriety for going aground at low water on the roof of the Underground tunnel at Carlton Place - an incident featured in the film "The Maggie".
Faithful 1906/70

The puffers would carry anything and go anywhere and they sailed into all sorts of places on the West coast. They would go where the bottom was reasonable and the tide would take them off again. The pufferman's ultimate humiliation was to be "neaped" - caught up a beach on a sequence of falling high tides. Here Hay's *Roman* has sailed up the burn at Blackwaterfoot on Arran.

Roman 1904/70

Scottish Malt Distillers owned two puffers, both named *Pibroch*, to take coal and malt to the island of Islay and to carry whisky from it. This is the second *Pibroch* and the Clyde's second diesel designed puffer. In general appearance she was very like the first diesel puffer, *Glenshira*; hardly surprising since they both came from the drawing board at Scott's of Bowling. The mini-van is taking advantage of her steel hatch covers (another first for the puffer trade) and avoiding the cost of the ferry and the road miles to Glasgow.

Pibroch 1956/120

Malt whisky from the Bunahabhain distillery on Islay would have been a typical return cargo for *Pibroch*. Until the late 1960s it was the main cargo for puffer companies like Hay and Ross and Marshall. The island exported over a million gallons of its world famous product annually through these companies, but this was to change dramatically in the 1970s when the ro-ro ferries took all the distillery trade.

Pibroch 1923/100

Ross and Marshall's *Stormlight* was the last steam puffer built for the West Highlands.
Stormlight had been intended as a motor vessel, following the example of Hamilton
and McPhail's successful *Glenshira*. However, her owners over-reacted to the Iranian
oil crisis and at the last moment had steam propulsion installed. Ten years later it was
almost impossible to engage stokers and she often languished unmanned.
Stormlight 1957/130

A Dutch puffer! *Druid* had been built in Papendracht in Holland in 1959 when Hay decided they wanted a 240 ton deadweight diesel ship for the West Highland trade. She was the last to carry Hay's series of "tribal" names. She was the only puffer to adopt a two derrick approach to discharging the long single cargo hatch that was a characteristic of the 240 tonners. Her capsize in the River Ribble in 1962, with the loss of her crew, was never satisfactorily explained.

Druid 1959/199

"Jacky". The spirit of Neil Munro's "Sunny Jim" shines from the eyes of this puffer's cabin boy.

The River's Royalty

The *Queen Mary* goes down the River for the first time in March 1936.

The high tide of the Clyde's prosperity as a shipping centre was in the twenty years before World War I - the last decade of Victoria's reign and the Edwardian era.

Britain was proud of its position on the world stage and of its Empire. The perception of Imperial greatness was certainly part of the public consciousness until the nation emerged somewhat battered from the War of 1939 to 1946. As the Scot put it, the nation had "a guid conceit o' itsel'".

Due deference was given to the position of the Head of State in this thinking and public loyalty and appreciation was expressed in the near mania for naming bridges, buildings, avenues, factories etc. after the Sovereign. Brave were the city fathers who did not find place for "Victoria", "Edward", "George", "Empire" or "Imperial" in the designation when it came to naming their latest public works. Even on what was to become known as "Red Clydeside" republican sentiment was put aside. As the Clyde developed the new docks were called "Queen's" (1880), "Prince's" (1897) and "King George V" (1931). Rothesay Dock (1907) would be the exception then? No. The premier peerage in Scotland, and a courtesy title of the monarch's eldest son, is the Dukedom of Rothesay.

Naming ships was no exception. Queen Victoria became Empress of India, at Disraeli's instigation in 1876, and

Unusually for one of the River's royal personages the *Queen Empress* was not a turbine steamer. But since her inspiration was likely to have been Victoria it was perhaps appropriate that she looked back to the days of reciprocating engines. Her modest speed and size (only just over eight feet of draft) did not preclude her from being sent to north Russia as a hospital ship in the 1914-18 War.

Queen Empress 1912/410

began to style herself "Regina et Imperator" thereafter. In 1912 a ship appeared on the Clyde, albeit a humble river paddler, called the *Queen Empress*. (Curiously, this was after the deaths of both Victoria and her son Edward VII.) She was, no doubt, at the time, the pride of her owners, John Williamson and Co. Ltd., and it was in their view both a compliment to the monarchy and a confirmation of their loyalty to it, to so name her. Just possibly, the cynics might say, it was also a marketing ploy to attract the public to the ship by the royal association.

Williamson was attracted to royalty as a theme for christening ships. He was part of the consortium which

developed Parson's turbine propulsion for commercial use and they named their revolutionary ship *King Edward*. (It was in 1901, the year of his ascending the throne.) She was the world's first turbine passenger steamer. The consortium, which included the shipbuilders Denny of Dumbarton, called themselves Turbine Steamers Ltd. to proclaim to the world their adoption of the new technology.

The newest technology must surely carry the titles of the highest in the land and, in 1902, when they built another ship to act as consort to the monarch on the Campbeltown route, she was named *Queen Alexandra*. Ten years later, after this Queen was badly damaged in a fire, a second

Queen Alexandra appeared. Twenty years later the consortium was still using the royal titles when it named its 1933 newbuilding *Queen Mary*. (She was soon to carry a suffix in deference to a somewhat larger ship.) Her consort, *King George V*, had appeared under the same house flag in 1926. And so in the world of the estuary's steamers the river had its royalty with the social order clearly established by the excellence of the technology, the speed of the craft and the elegance of their design.

In the annals of the Clyde the story of John Brown's newbuilding *No. 534* is too well known to be repeated in great detail here. Her keel was laid down in 1930 but work on her was halted due to the recession and the financial difficulties of her would-be owners, Cunard. For nearly two years no further work was done on her but the Government of the day eventually advanced £3 million on the condition that Cunard and the White Star Line (which was virtually insolvent) amalgamated their Trans-Atlantic interests. *No. 534* was launched in September 1933 as the *Queen Mary*. The request that she might be so named had been made in writing by the builders to Buckingham Palace in advance of the launch.

Now the Clyde had two royal ladies of the same name. Both were turbine driven so the new ship did qualify in a way to be included in the River's established royalty. Clearly 81,000 gross tons carried more weight than 870, a length of 1019 feet was more compelling than one of 263 and the Cunarder had the advantage of being launched by the lady herself. So the Turbine Steamers' management deferred to size and sentiment and agreed to add a suffix to their ship's name. She became *Queen Mary II*.

The Government's support of the Cunard-White Star Line required that a second trans-Atlantic liner was built. *No. 552* went on the same slip at Clydebank that had carried the *Queen Mary* and in 1938 her slightly bigger sister, the *Queen Elizabeth* (83,000 gross tons), took to the water. She was sent on her way by her namesake.

By 1958 more people were crossing the Atlantic by air than by sea and those liners that survived looked to the cruising tourist for their livelihood. By 1968 both Queens had been retired. The *Queen Elizabeth* burnt out and sank at Hong Kong in 1972 but the *Queen Mary* still serves as an hotel and tourist attraction in California.

The last of the Clyde's great liners was to be the *Queen Elizabeth 2*. A luxury cruise ship rather than a trans-Atlantic greyhound, she was dogged by technical difficulties with her turbines after her 1967 launch. She was delivered to her owners in 1969, nearly a year late. She reputedly lost her builders £1 million - a symptom of the general decline of British shipbuilding? However, she sails on successfully today, an instantly recognisable presence in the ports of the world and the last of the line of the River's royalty.

The *King Edward* was the world's first commercial turbine steamer.

A syndicate of Denny of Dumbarton, Parson (the inventor of the marine turbine) and local shipowner, Capt. John Williamson, had her built for the Fairlie to Campbeltown service.

Denny, with an eye to future business, contributed over 70% of the cost. She proved to be much faster, if a little more expensive in fuel, than paddle ships of similar size. Shipowners were impressed and the orders rolled in.

She served in the Clyde until 1952 and was requisitioned by the Admiralty in both Wars. (She took troops to Archangel in the 1914-18 conflict.)

When she was broken up in 1952 her unique turbine engine was preserved in Glasgow's Museum of Transport.

King Edward 1901/640

The Queen who became a Saint. This is not Scotland's Queen Margaret but King Edward VII's Consort who was canonised by MacBrayne. This, the second *Queen Alexandra* was produced by Denny as a replacement for the 1902 vessel and operated for Turbine Steamers Ltd. on the fast run from Greenock to Campbeltown. She acquired a reputation to rival another queen - Boadicea - when she rammed and sank a submarine in the 1914-1918 War.

When MacBrayne took over Turbine Steamers in 1935 this ship went with the sale and emerged from a refit much altered as the *St Columba*. An enlarged saloon, a second mast and a third funnel went with the sainthood.

She was broken up in 1959 after a quiet World War II and post war service in the Clyde estuary.

St Columba 1912/850

As son follows father it was perhaps inevitable that the *King George V* would be a Denny turbine steamer. She lasted for nearly fifty years and under MacBrayne's ownership she ran from Oban to Iona and Staffa in the summer months.

She had been built for Turbine Steamers Ltd. and she had opened King George V Dock in 1931 by repeating the ribbon breaking ceremony that marked the inauguration of Rothesay Dock by the *Duchess of Rothesay* in 1907. By that time the Duke of Rothesay of 1907 had become the fifth George to sit on the throne of the United Kingdom.

King George V 1926/990

This 1974 picture of *Queen Mary II* shows her leaving Tighnabruaich pier in the Kyles of Bute. Within five years she was laid up as the demand for the type of "day trip" work that she was then involved in had decreased.

She was converted from coal to oil burning when in her twenties and in the process lost one of her two funnels. Under her original Wiiliamson-Buchanan ownership she had gracefully adopted the suffix "II" in deference to the larger Cunarder which followed her down the slips a year later in 1934. Perhaps for that sentimental reason she was purchased by Glasgow District as a living example of the great days of Clyde steamer building. Plans for her renovation were abandoned in the welter of public spending reductions that characterised the 1980s.

Queen Mary II 1933/1,010

The sheer mass of the *Queen Mary* is put into context by the size of the human figures in the field on the south bank of the River - a mile away from the slipway. It is early in September 1934 and by the end of the month she will be launched.

The crowds gather expectantly on the south bank of the River to watch the *Queen Mary* leave Brown's and make her way to the open sea; clear evidence of the interest and pride of the Clydesiders in the achievements of their River and the significance to them all that this particular ship was completed.

The keel of Yard *No. 534* was laid at the end of 1930 but work on her was stopped in 1931 because recession-struck Cunard could not afford to complete her. Great economic hardship followed for Clydeside. Cunard's great rival, the White Star Line, was also in a straitened financial condition and the Government of the day forced through a merger of the two and subsidised the restart of her construction.

Queen Mary 1934/81,200

Back in the Clyde for the last time. In 1966 *Queen Elizabeth* was docked at Greenock for inspection at what was almost the end of the era of the great liners. Fifteen months later the loss-making *Queen Mary* was to be sold and the *Elizabeth* was keeping the New York service open with the French Lines' *France* as a running mate. Sold in 1968, she passed through several hands before the final indignity of burning out and being scrapped in Hong Kong in 1972.

Queen Elizabeth 1938/83,700

The *Queen Elizabeth 2*, seen here before her September 1967 launch, was designed with an eye to the world cruising market as well as the replacement of the ageing transatlantic Queens. This was just as well for it was the cruising market which grew.

Queen Elizabeth 2 1967/67,100

Alas, the problems of forecasting the new ship's market were reflected ashore. *Queen Elizabeth 2* was nearly a year late in being delivered because of problems with her Clyde-built turbines. She reputedly lost John Brown's a million pounds of her £29 million building cost.

Queen Elizabeth 2 1967/67,100

The great ship is soon to leave her birthplace. Before her lay thirty-one years of service in war and peace, a Blue Riband for an average speed of 31 knots and one thousand Atlantic crossings. She survives to this day as a hotel and conference centre at Long Beach, California, USA.

Queen Mary 1934/81,200

"Bless Them All"

the long and the short.

Nothing quite sums up the complete range of the Clyde's shipbuilding output as does this photograph of the sixty-six foot puffer *Serb* steaming past the one thousand and twenty-nine feet of the *Queen Elizabeth* on her building berth. Bless them all.